Classics and Prison Education in the US

This volume focuses on teaching Classics in carceral contexts in the US and offers an overview of the range of incarcerated adults, their circumstances, and the ways in which they are approaching and reinterpreting Greek and Roman texts.

Classics and Prison Education in the US examines how different incarcerated adults – male, female, or gender non-conforming; young or old; serving long sentences or about to be released – are reading and discussing Classical texts, and what this may entail. Moreover, it provides a sophisticated examination of the best pedagogical practices for teaching in a prison setting and for preparing returning citizens, as well as a considered discussion of the possible dangers of engaging in such teaching – whether because of the potential complicity with the carceral state, or because of the historical position of Classics in elitist education.

This edited volume will be a resource for those interested in Classics pedagogy, as well as the role that Classics can play in different areas of society and education, and the impact it can have.

Emilio Capettini is Assistant Professor of Classics at the University of California, Santa Barbara. His scholarly work has appeared in *Materiali e discussioni per l'analisi dei testi classici, Classical Quarterly, Mnemosyne*, and the *American Journal of Philology*.

Nancy Sorkin Rabinowitz is Professor Emerita of Comparative Literature at Hamilton College. Her publications include *Anxiety Veiled: Euripides and the Traffic in Women* (1993), *Greek Tragedy* (2008), and many co-edited volumes, including *Sex in Antiquity* (2014) and *From Abortion to Pederasty: Addressing Difficult Topics in the Classics Classroom* (2014).

Classics In and Out of the Academy
Classical Pedagogy in the Twenty-First Century
Series editors – Fiona McHardy and Nancy Rabinowitz

This series of short volumes explores the ways in which the study of antiquity can enrich the lives of diverse populations in the twenty-first century. The series covers two distinct, but interrelated topics: (1) ways in which classicists can engage new audiences within the profession by embedding inclusivity and diversity in school and university teaching practices, curricula, and assessments and (2) the relevance of Classics to learners from the most marginalized social strata (e.g. the incarcerated, refugees, those suffering from mental illness).

Classics and Prison Education in the US
Edited by Emilio Capettini and Nancy Sorkin Rabinowitz

Classics and Prison Education in the US

Edited by
Emilio Capettini and
Nancy Sorkin Rabinowitz

Routledge
Taylor & Francis Group

LONDON AND NEW YORK

First published 2021
by Routledge
2 Park Square, Milton Park, Abingdon, Oxon OX14 4RN

and by Routledge
605 Third Avenue, New York, NY 10158

Routledge is an imprint of the Taylor & Francis Group, an informa business

British Library Cataloguing-in-Publication Data
A catalogue record for this book is available from the British Library

Library of Congress Cataloging-in-Publication Data
Names: Capettini, Emilio, editor. | Rabinowitz, Nancy Sorkin, editor.
Title: Classics and prison education in the US / edited by Emilio Capettini and Nancy Sorkin Rabinowitz.
Other titles: Classics in and out of the academy.
Description: Abingdon, Oxon ; New York, NY: Routledge, 2021. | Series: Classics in and out of the academy : classical pedagogy in the twenty-first century | Includes bibliographical references and index. |
Identifiers: LCCN 2020055406 (print) | LCCN 2020055407 (ebook) | ISBN 9780367820619 (hardback) | ISBN 9781032011943 (paperback) | ISBN 9781003018629 (ebook)
Subjects: LCSH: Prisoners--Education--United States. | Classical literature--Study and teaching--United States.
Classification: LCC HV8883.3.U5 C53 2021 (print) | LCC HV8883.3.U5 (ebook) | DDC 374.1826/9270973--dc23
LC record available at https://lccn.loc.gov/2020055406
LC ebook record available at https://lccn.loc.gov/2020055407

ISBN: 978-0-367-82061-9 (hbk)
ISBN: 978-1-032-01194-3 (pbk)
ISBN: 978-1-003-01862-9 (ebk)

Typeset in Times New Roman
by MPS Limited, Dehradun

Contents

Contributors

Emily Allen-Hornblower is Associate Professor of Classics at Rutgers University. Her book (*From Agent to Spectator: Witnessing the Aftermath in Ancient Greek Epic and Tragedy*, 2016) and articles center on ancient (and modern) portrayals of the human condition, and factors of connection (and disconnection) between individuals and groups. Allen-Hornblower teaches in prisons through NJ-STEP.

Elizabeth Bobrick is Visiting Scholar in the Department of Classical Studies of Wesleyan University, where she has taught ancient Greek language and literature; she has also been Visiting Writer in the Department of English, where she taught creative nonfiction. She has published on Aristophanes, Theophrastus, and Sophocles, and her non-scholarly work has appeared in *Salon*, *Creative Nonfiction*, *Women's Review of Books*, *The Conversation*, and elsewhere. Wesleyan's Center for Prison Education (https://www.wesleyan.edu/cpe/) sponsored her teaching at Cheshire Correctional Institution for men, and at York Correctional Institute for women.

Emilio Capettini is Assistant Professor of Classics at the University of California, Santa Barbara. His research focuses on Greek literature of the imperial period and on classical reception. He has taught Latin through the Prison Teaching Initiative at Princeton University.

Nicole Dib is Assistant Professor of English at Southern Utah University. She completed her Ph.D. in contemporary multi-ethnic American literature at the University of California, Santa Barbara, in 2020, where she worked as Teaching Fellow for the "Foundations in the Humanities" prison correspondence course. Her scholarly work has appeared or is forthcoming in *MELUS: Multiethnic Literature of the United States*, *The Routledge*

Companion to Critical Masculinity Studies, and *Feminism and Comics: New Essays on Interpretation.*

Elena Dugan is Postgraduate Research Associate in the Religion Department at Princeton University, researching the texts and traditions of early Judaism, Christianity, and Islam. She has taught and tutored in three prisons in New Jersey.

Olga Faccani is a doctoral candidate in the Department of Classics at the University of California, Santa Barbara, where she worked as Teaching Fellow for the "Foundations in the Humanities" prison correspondence course. Her current research focuses on Greek drama, storytelling, and affective bonds among characters on stage. At UC Santa Barbara, she also collaborates with The Odyssey Project, a theater process between youth from a juvenile detention facility in Santa Barbara county and UC undergraduate students.

Nancy Felson is Professor Emerita of Classics at the University of Georgia, where she taught Greek poetry, mythology, gender studies, and Latin poetry. She has served as Whitehead Professor at the ASCSA in Athens, Greece, and as instructor in the Bard Prison Initiative (BPI). Her research involves applying tools from narratology, semiotics, pragmatics, gender studies, and linguistics to the understanding of Homeric epic, Pindar's victory odes, and Greek tragedy. She has published *Regarding Penelope: From Character to Poetics* (1994) and is a participant in "Performing Pindar" with Helen Eastman and Alex Silverman.

Amy E. Johnson has taught in Columbia University's Justice-in-Education Initiative and in the Humanities Core program, and most recently in NYU's Prison Education Program, both in the US. Her monograph, *Theocritean Pastoral: A Study in the Definition of Genre*, was recently published (2020).

Michael Morgan is Teaching Professor at the University of California, Santa Barbara. He is a designated Linklater teacher, a lead trainer at the Fitzmaurice Institute, and the author of *Constructing the Holistic Actor: Fitzmaurice Voicework* (2008).

Dan-el Padilla Peralta is Associate Professor of Classics at Princeton University. He is the author of *Undocumented: A Dominican Boy's Odyssey from a Homeless Shelter to the Ivy League* (2015) and *Divine Institutions: Religions and Community in the Middle Roman Republic* (2020).

Alexandra Pappas is Associate Professor and Raoul Bertrand Chair in Classics at San Francisco State University, where she has been since 2012. Her research and publications have broadly explored how ancient Greek words and images make meaning together. She has been a member of *The Medea Project: Theatre for Incarcerated Women/HIV Circle* since 2016.

Zachary Price is Assistant Professor of Doctoral Studies in the Department of Drama at the University of California, Irvine. He is the author of the forthcoming monograph *Black Dragon: Afro Asian Performance and the Martial Arts Imagination*. His publications have also appeared in *Theatre Topics*, *The Drama Review*, *The National Review of Black Politics*, *Journal of Asian American Studies*, and *The Postcolonialist*.

Nancy Sorkin Rabinowitz is Professor Emerita of Comparative Literature at Hamilton College. Her work centers on Greek tragedy, and Classics and social justice. She is the author of *Anxiety Veiled: Euripides and the Traffic in Women* (1993) and *Greek Tragedy* (2008), and has edited many volumes of essays, including *Sex in Antiquity* (with Mark Masterson and James Robson, 2014) and *From Abortion to Pederasty: Addressing Difficult Topics in the Classics Classroom* (with Fiona McHardy, 2014). Her current scholarly work is on same-sex desire in the House of Atreus myth.

Stephen Scully is Professor of Classical Studies at Boston University. He writes on Greek and Latin Literature, translation, and reception, with books on Homer and Hesiod, and translations of Euripides' *Suppliant Women* (with Rosanna Warren) and Plato's *Phaedrus*.

Laura M. Slatkin teaches both at NYU's Gallatin School and in the NYU Prison Education Program in the US. She is Visiting Professor in the Committee on Social Thought at the University of Chicago.

Nebojša Todorović is a doctoral candidate in Comparative Literature at Yale University. His dissertation (provisionally entitled *Traumatic Cartographies: Greek Tragedy Across the Adriatic*) traces the reception of classical Greek tragedies in the post-conflict contexts of the "greater Balkans" in the late twentieth and early twenty-first centuries. Todorović taught an Introductory Latin class for the Yale Prison Education Initiative in Summer of

2019 and plans to offer language and literature classes for YPEI in the near future.

Mathura Umachandran is Mellon Postdoctoral Fellow in the Society for the Humanities and Visiting Lecturer in the Department of Classics at Cornell University. Her research is broadly within classical reception, ranging between critical theory, critical race studies, and contemporary art. She has taught Latin and Classical Mythology in prisons in New Jersey.

Jessica Wright has taught through the Prison Teaching Initiative at Princeton University and the Philosophy and Literature Circle at the University of Texas at San Antonio, where she was previously Assistant Professor of Classics and Medical Humanities. She is currently Teaching Associate at the University of Sheffield. Her publications include "Latin Behind Bars: Teaching College Latin in an American Prison" (*Eidolon*, 2017) and "Talking to Strangers (in Latin): Teaching Latin in the Prison Classroom" (*Cloelia*, 2017).

Introduction

Emilio Capettini and
Nancy Sorkin Rabinowitz

This volume on teaching Classics in prison settings comes for the most part from presentations delivered at several conferences – at the Society for Classical Studies, the Classical Association of the Atlantic States, and the University of California, Santa Barbara Interdisciplinary Humanities Center Symposium on Humanities in Prison. The editors and contributors are grateful to those organizations and the audiences for their generous responses, which inspired this project.

Those presentations, and the lively discussions that followed them, are a testament to the current interest in the topic, an interest galvanized by an increasing awareness of the US prison problem. The exponential rise of rates of incarceration in the US since the 1970s has given new meaning to the idea of American exceptionalism: with 4% of the global population, the US has nearly 25% of the world's prison population. As is by now well known, this situation is starkly racialized: Black men are six times more likely to be arrested than white men, and Black and Latinx boys are more likely to go to jail than to college (much less to graduate from one). What might not be as widely recognized is that this pressing issue cuts across gender distinctions: according to a recent report by the ACLU, women are the fastest-growing segment of the incarcerated population in the US.[1] Although far from painting a complete picture, these statistics and data allow one to gauge the toll that mass incarceration exerts – both emotionally and economically – on communities across this country. Ironically, this system is extremely expensive to maintain: its cost for taxpayers is around $80 billion annually, in spite of the fact that incarcerated individuals work for almost nothing, eat substandard food, and survive in dehumanizing, crowded surroundings – a situation that has been exacerbated even further by the COVID-19 pandemic.[2]

What is to be done about this enormous problem? A proposal that has been gaining more and more support in recent years is that of abolishing prisons entirely. The choice of the term abolition is not casual: Angela Davis, who is a major voice in favor of this position, has been using this word to highlight, as explicitly as possible, the connection of the prison system to slavery, and scholars and activists have increasingly traced the racism of the modern carceral system back to the period immediately after the formal abolition of slavery. As their work has made clear, slavery did not end with the 13th amendment – and not simply because its text contained a provision for "involuntary servitude" as punishment for a crime. The Black codes and vagrancy laws which were passed to police the formerly enslaved established a new system of peonage (Davis 1998, 75–6; Alexander 2010, 28–32; Blackamon 2008, 53–7); imprisoned for vagrancy, which in most cases simply meant that they were unemployed, Black men would become a new penal work force in what was, in all but name, a legal continuation of slavery. In this way, incarceration provided the labor for the convict lease system that was essential for the continued profitability of the plantations and the success of later industry in the post-bellum South (Smith and Hattery 2008, 85; Blackamon 2008, 45–53).

The pernicious legacy of slavery has also been linked with the expansion of the US prison system in recent decades: in her well-known 2010 book, Michelle Alexander has described the mass incarceration fueled by the war on drugs as "the New Jim Crow," an institution designed to continue segregation and the oppression of people of color.[3] Given this context, it is hardly surprising that Davis has repeatedly called into question the supposed usefulness of prisons and argued that their very existence "relieves us of the responsibility of seriously engaging with the problems of our society, especially those produced by racism and, increasingly, global capitalism" (Davis 2003, 16). Incarceration is, in her view, "the punitive solution to a whole range of social problems that are not being addressed" (Davis 2005, 40). The abolition of prisons would, then, force us to reckon with the systemic and pressing problems of our society and to enact real change.

This radical position is not for everyone, however, and, even if the public debate were to shift in favor of abolition, the process could not take place overnight. What could and should be done in the meantime? Prison education has emerged as one of the most common ways in which people who recognize the problems of mass incarceration attempt to have an impact. After the Congress' 1994 decision to make incarcerated students ineligible for Pell Grants, many college-in-prison programs that had been created in the 1970s and the 1980s closed; since then, volunteer efforts and initiatives by private institutions have tried to ensure that incarcerated individuals continue to have access not just to vocational training but also to college-level instruction.

This volume sets out the various ways in which Classicists have joined these endeavors whether by co-teaching Humanities courses with colleagues from related disciplines or by offering classes entirely focused on ancient cultures, literatures, and languages. What has been done thus far? What have been the pitfalls? What do we need to be mindful of going forward? In the essays gathered here, teachers at various stages of their academic careers – from graduate students to full professors – reflect on their experiences teaching Classics or Classics-related courses in carceral settings. Some of them take a more narrative tone, as they guide the reader through the process of devising and designing their course and explain which of their expectations were confirmed, which upended once instruction began. Others adopt more theoretical approaches using the knowledge they acquired in their interactions with incarcerated or formerly incarcerated students to examine the challenges of prison education. Collectively, the essays in this volume offer an overview of the range of incarcerated in-dividuals – male, female, or gender non-conforming; young or old; serving long sentences or about to be released – who are reading and discussing Greek and Roman texts, and of the different ways in which they are approaching and reinterpreting them. No less importantly, they provide a sophisticated examination of the best pedagogical practices for teaching in a prison setting and for preparing returning citizens, as well as a considered discussion of the possible dangers of engaging in such teaching.

We have organized the essays into three sections: the first focuses primarily on the ways in which Classics courses that are offered on college campuses have been reconfigured for in-person instruction in carceral settings; the second examines interactions with students and approaches to the texts that might be less familiar to some instructors, such as those that use correspondence or theatrical production as the primary mode of interaction; the third and last takes a critical ap-proach to prison education and the role of Classics within it. As might be expected, however, there are some questions and concerns that connect all the essays in the volume, regardless of the sections in which they appear. In what follows, we will foreground two among these shared concerns – one specific to the discipline of Classics, the other connected with prison education projects more broadly.

The first important element upon which all the essays reflect is the value of teaching Greco-Roman literature and culture to students en-tangled within the carceral system – be they in prison or recently released. Pondering (and questioning) the role that Greek and Roman antiquity can still play in our world has always been important for Classicists, who are frequently asked to make a case for the continued relevance of their discipline.[4] In recent years, with the rise of social justice movements, Classics' implication in systems of oppression and its historical function as a gatekeeping tool, hindering the social advancement of marginalized groups, have been increasingly explored and scrutinized.[5] In this context, the risk of "instrumentalizing our [incarcerated] students toward the renewal of our discipline," as Wright aptly puts it in her essay, becomes apparent, and examining whether, and to what extent, they found meaning and value in the study of ancient Greek and Roman materials emerges as all the more urgent.

Many of the essays in this volume detail how deeply ancient texts can resonate with students who are or have been incarcerated, enabling them to reflect on their experiences at a distance, as it were. For instance, cis and trans women in the San Francisco County Jail, incarcerated youth in the Santa Barbara Department of Youth Probation's Los Prietos Boys Camp, and men in a medium-security NY State Correctional Facility – as Pappas, Morgan and Price, and Johnson and Slatkin explain in their essays – all felt a deep affinity with Odysseus and found in his adventures a useful model for thinking about the trajectory of their lives and their own homecoming. The *Odyssey* also prompted students to ponder the meaning of heroism and reflect on different ideals of masculinity; as Felson reports in her conversation with Todorović, the men enrolled in one of the courses she taught as part of the Bard Prison Initiative engaged in passionate discussions while contrasting Telemachus' maturation in the *Odyssey* with that of Achilles in the *Iliad*. Moreover, the concepts of honor and glory that are central to many archaic Greek texts allowed several students to establish connections between the content of their classes and their lived experiences both inside and outside carceral spaces. Bobrick points out that the "inseparable combination of status, material goods, and control of territory" conveyed by the Greek term *timē* (which is roughly equivalent to "honor" and "respect") appeared familiar to some of her students as they discussed the *Homeric Hymn to Demeter*. Similarly, Padilla Peralta explains that the deep ambivalence of Hector's speech to Andromache in Book 6 of the *Iliad* – a speech in which Hector pits his wife's requests against his fear of being shamed in front of the Trojans and his desire to win glory – reminded one of the returning citizens who participated in Columbia University's Justice-in-Education Initiative of "the mentality of street gangs."

As one might expect, texts by Aeschylus, Sophocles, and Euripides also elicited vivid, intense, and at times unexpected reactions. Johnson and Slatkin detail, for instance, not only how horrified the men in their classes were by the sacrifice of Iphigenia in the *Agamemnon* and how gripped they felt by Ajax's plight in Sophocles' play, but also how reluctant they proved, at first, to sympathize with Antigone, a female character, within the public space of the classroom. Felson and Todorović examine how the *Philoctetes* enabled students to deepen the examination of different instantiations of masculinity and fatherhood that they had begun while reading the Homeric poems. And Allen-Hornblower explains how tragedies such as *Medea, Ajax, Heracles,* and *Philoctetes* allowed her and her students to meditate upon the forms that heroism can take in everyday life and to engage in a careful examination of the cognitive basis of positive and negative emotions and of the ranges of outcomes they can lead to.

Yet even texts that might not be at the very top of an instructor's list as they are planning a prison class for the first time deeply resonated with incarcerated students. Dib and Faccani discuss how, in the correspondence course for which they served as instructors, the story of Philemon and Baucis told by Ovid in Book 8 of the *Metamorphoses* prompted students to craft written reflections on the meaning of kindness, sacrifice, and punishment, as well as on the connections between the ancient text and their experiences, that went well beyond what had been required of them.

Because of the strict limitations that many carceral institutions have placed on the circulation and publication of the work of incarcerated individuals, most of the reactions and responses to ancient texts mentioned above are reported by the instructors rather than described by the students in their own words. However, at least some of the contributors – Allen-Hornblower, Pappas, and Johnson and Slatkin – have been allowed to include short remarks by their students about the courses they attended. Even in their brevity, these comments show how the discussions that took place in these prison classrooms developed traditional conversations in new directions, and allow one to understand fully why several of the contributors describe the interactions with their students as illuminating, thought-provoking, and energizing.

This does not mean, however, that Greek and Roman texts are endowed with some sort of universality that makes them easily transferable from one classroom to the other or equally appealing to different groups of students, regardless of their backgrounds, lived experiences, or aspirations. Particularly instructive in this regard is an incident related by Scully in his essay: one of the students enrolled in a mythology course that he taught in a medium-security prison in the

1980s fervently hated the *Odyssey*, deeming it nothing other than a work of propaganda meant to extol western imperialism. Perhaps less trenchant but just as significant was the reaction of a student in a much more recent mythology course, one taught by Dugan and Umachandran in a NJ prison in 2017. When presented with the syllabus for the class, this student pointedly asked: "Isn't this all white man's mythology?" These reactions – no less important than those detailed in other essays – are a powerful reminder of the dialogues, challenges, and negotiations that are bound to take place between students and instructors during any course. Yet they also (and most significantly) highlight how essential it is for Classicists to ponder carefully the best ways to introduce in the prison classroom texts that have often been wielded as tools of exclusion or used to promote colonialist projects.

These pedagogical concerns represent the second major *fil rouge* running through the volume. All the contributors highlight the importance of creating and fostering a space in which individuals who are (or have been) dehumanized and subjected to physical or psychological violence in the prison can feel safe and empowered to voice their opinions. In their conversation about the *Odyssey Project*, for instance, Price and Morgan discuss the importance of listening to incarcerated youths and of helping them to liberate their voices both literally – as they prepare to perform in front of an audience their own rewritings of Odysseus' adventures – and metaphorically – as they strive to express who they are and what they hope to achieve. Similarly, Padilla Peralta emphasizes how essential active listening and sensitivity to trauma proved to be during his interactions with formerly incarcerated students, and explains how he strove to "inspire [them] to pursue therapeutic interpretations, at their own pace and inclination." And a comparable approach is articulated by Felson and Todorović, who argue that the dialogic pedagogy of Paulo Freire provides an important model for building knowledge within the prison classroom, one in which teachers and students share resources and experiences.

Creating such a space within carceral settings is, of course, no easy task, and some of the essays in the volume examine the dangers of which Classicists and prison educators more generally must be aware. Dugan and Umachandran warn, for instance, of the risk of replicating within the prison classroom exclusionary practices – for example, those concerning linguistic competency – that are typical of more traditional academic settings. Moreover, they emphasize that even the most sincere commitment to a pedagogy that foregrounds equality between instructors and students cannot erase the power imbalances that are an integral component of the prison system. Pappas, too, encourages prospective and current prison teachers to be keenly aware of their privilege and power, and urges them to strive to find ways to promote the voices of the students instead of speaking on their behalf. Last but not least – in what is a fitting conclusion to the volume – Wright examines the limitations and pitfalls of the most prevalent narratives in support of prison education, and outlines a set of strategies, grounded in self-reflexivity and mutual accountability, for Classicists to follow in order to ensure that their contributions to prison education truly promote social justice.

No single formula can be offered for the success of Classics-based prison courses. What the essays gathered here make clear, however, is the importance of creating a learning environment in which incarcerated or recently released individuals are reminded and reassured that, as a student enrolled in one of the classes that Nancy taught put it, they "can still make a contribution to humanity whether inside or outside." Many suggestions on how to achieve this essential but elusive goal are presented in the pages that follow; yet we would like to think of the observations offered by this volume as the starting point of a long and fruitful conversation. Readers, we hope, will imagine ways forward that are still to be explored.

Notes

1 https://www.aclu.org/issues/smart-justice/mass-incarceration.
2 As of July 2020, the rate of infection in prison was 5.5 times that of the general population; cf. Saloner et al. 2020. For continuing coverage of these issues, see https://www.themarshallproject.org/2020/05/01/a-state-by-state-look-at-coronavirus-in-prisons. The pandemic has shut down for the past year most prison teaching, although the correspondence course model has helped some programs to continue.
3 While recognizing the factual basis and popular appeal of Alexander's ideas, other intellectuals – for instance, Ruth Wilson Gilmore – have cautioned against focusing entirely on nonviolent drug offenders – the "relatively innocent," in Gilmore's phrase – or strengthening the assumption that mass incarceration is purely a "Black problem," and have argued for the need to formulate pro-abolition arguments that do not shy away from the ethical and social complexity of the issue at hand. On Gilmore's views, see Kushner 2019.
4 For a recent examination of the issue of value for Classicists, see The Postclassicisms Collective 2019, 8–18.
5 On Classics and colonialism, see, e.g., Goff 2005 and Vasunia 2013.

Works cited

Alexander, Michelle. 2010. *The New Jim Crow: Mass Incarceration in the Age of Colorblindness*. New York: New Press.

Blackamon, Douglas A. 2008. *Slavery by Another Name: The Re-enslavement of Black Americans from the Civil War to World War II*. New York: Doubleday.

Davis, Angela Y. 1998. "From the Prison of Slavery to the Slavery of Prison: Frederick Douglass and the Convict Lease System." In *The Angela Y. Davis Reader*, edited by Joy James, 74–95. Malden, Mass: Blackwell.

Davis, Angela Y. 2003. *Are Prisons Obsolete?* New York: Seven Stories Press.

Davis, Angela Y. 2005. *Abolition Democracy: Beyond Empire, Prisons, and Torture*. New York: Seven Stories Press.

Goff, Barbara E., ed. 2005. *Classics and Colonialism*. London: Duckworth.

Kushner, Rachel. 2019. "Is Prison Necessary? Ruth Wilson Gilmore Might Change Your Mind." *The New York Times Magazine*, April 17, 2019. https://www.nytimes.com/2019/04/17/magazine/prison-abolition-ruth-wilson-gilmore.html.

Saloner, Brendan, Kalind Parish, Julie A. Ward, Grace DiLaura, and Sharon Dolovich. 2020. "COVID-19 Cases and Deaths in Federal and State Prisons." *JAMA* 324 (6): 602–603. https://jamanetwork.com/journals/jama/fullarticle/2768249.

Smith, Earl, and Angela J. Hattery. 2008. "Incarceration: A Tool for Racial Segregation and Labor Exploitation." *Race, Gender & Class* 15 (1–2): 79–97.

The Postclassicisms Collective. 2019. *Postclassicisms*. Chicago and London: The University of Chicago Press.

Vasunia, Phiroze. 2013. *The Classics and Colonial India*. Oxford: Oxford University Press.

Part I
Old texts, new classrooms

1 Reading the emotions inside and outside: classical Greek texts in prison and beyond

Emily Allen-Hornblower

Rikers Island. There is a man locked in his cell, banging the metal door with a cup, swearing and screaming. Other inmates are milling about the panopticon, but he has been confined to his cell. The correctional officers (COs) curse him out. Other inmates curse him out. To no avail. He's making as much noise as he can, and his anger and frustration are palpable. I have just arrived in one of the jails ("housing units") at Rikers Island, along with a group of actors, to perform a version (abridged) of Euripides' *Trojan Women*, as preface to a conversation with the incarcerated men of that unit. I organized the event – the first of a series – with the support of a Whiting Seed Grant in Public Engagement, as well as the Just One Foundation (more on these events later).[1] The visit was made possible thanks to an initiative to bring the visual and performing arts into New York correctional facilities in a more systematic way, spearheaded by one man: Tommy Demenkoff.[2] Our event, we found out on arrival, was to be held in the Mental Observation Unit (MOU), where most of the men were wandering around their section of the panopticon with a lost look on their faces – some, we later discovered, knew close to no English. The man in his cell continued screaming right up until I began with some introductory remarks and background information about the Trojan War. My goal was to contextualize the play for the dozen or so prisoners who drifted around us, intrigued. Some came closer, sat down at tables or hovered close by for the entire performance. One even lay down on the ground in front of the actors, cupping his head in his hands. From the moment we started, the man in his cell stopped yelling. I could see him on the upper balcony row, his face pressed hard against the window-like opening of bars that provided a small lookout onto the inside of the panopticon through his cell door. He remained quiet throughout the performance and discussion – except when a group of COs yelled mid-play, "Medication, *so and so!*" over and over, once for each individual being administered medication. At that point, he shouted: "Shut the F*ck up! We're trying to watch a f*cking play here!"

This man's rage and entranced silence are as moving as they are unsettling a tribute to the power of theater and the Humanities. His response raises many essential points regarding the place of the Liberal Arts within our curricula; indeed, it touches on the place and role of the Arts and of Literature in our lives, and in our education – including, in this case, behind bars. Why and how did a play speak to this man when nothing and no one else had until then? Brutality and coercion did nothing for him; Euripides' drama did. Was there something calming, even therapeutic (dare I say cathartic?) about watching Greek tragedy in performance – something in the words, the movements of the actors, or the cadence of the Chorus's collective chants? The moment points in the starkest possible terms to the Humanities' and Liberal Arts' necessary and crucial place in every education. Reading, writing, or, in this case, viewing and hearing historical texts and literature in prison is not a luxury; neither is thinking about nor making Art. It is, rather, "a question of survival," in the words of Jesse Krimes, a reentering citizen who spoke about the art he made while he served time.[3] "It is about our dignity," said Joseph Rodriguez, another formerly incarcerated man and avid photographer.

The MOU men with whom I discussed Euripides at Rikers were not my students. This was a "cold" visit, not part of a more extensive educational program. I had never been inside this housing unit before, nor met the individuals with whom we considered these texts. I was discouraged from getting any names, so I am unable to attribute any quotes; I can only relate some of their words and reactions. One of the men, the one who lay down on the floor in front of the performers, asked: "So ... was all of this Zeus?" Indeed, that is precisely what the Trojan women state at the close of the play, as the walls of Troy crumble. To this he responded, "That damn m*ther f*cker started up all this bullsh*t and then just f*cking took off?" This man, who had been placed in the MOU of a Rikers jail, went straight to the existential question posed by countless suffering characters of Greek tragedy: after a desperate call to the gods to witness human suffering ("Zeus, are you seeing this?") goes unanswered, the painful realization hits home: despite manifest divine indifference, "none of these things is not Zeus."[4] It later struck me: *mutatis mutandis,* if we replace Zeus with Society in this man's words, the applicability of his statement to mass incarceration rings painfully true. We, as a society, fail the most vulnerable among us in countless realms, not least in the crucial realms of education, opportunity, and our penal system. We create this morass – and then we just … warehouse them and take off.

The visit to Rikers was a one-day gig and an outlier in that respect. The teaching I have done behind bars since 2015 has otherwise been for a full semester, as the sole instructor for a number of for-credit college courses on literature, history and culture (often ancient Greek), in two different men's prisons in New Jersey: Northern State Prison (NSP, medium-security), and East Jersey State Prison (EJSP, maximum-security) in Rahway. I first learned about the possibility of teaching college courses behind bars somewhat by chance, when reading an interview of a student, Chris Etienne, in Rutgers' *Daily Targum*. Etienne was pursuing an undergraduate education through Rutgers' Mountainview Program after doing some time, and also going back to tutor his former peers behind bars.[5] We met. I found out I could teach behind bars through NJ-STEP (Scholarship and Transformative Education in Prisons). I have taught several semesters since then – in the summer, early mornings, or at night.[6]

The men I have taught range in age from their 20's to late 60's. Roughly 90% are African-American. The length of their sentences varies; many are several decades long (my courses have mostly been offered at a maximum-security prison). The students are like other students in all fundamental ways, working diligently towards their degree, albeit with an especially noteworthy drive and pride in their education. Their dedication and passionate intellectual engagement with the material are all the more remarkable given their circumstances.[7] They must overcome countless obstacles simply to read, write, think, and study, including sheer noise; limited access to materials outside of class (no computers or Internet; very limited access to books); and limited materials within our classrooms (a board; DOC pre-approved handouts, books, and images). Their resilience and ability to maintain focus and a sense of purpose in the face of a chaotic daily life of constant disruptions – not to mention sometimes dire news regarding denied appeals – are an awe-inspiring testament to the human spirit.

Each class usually has just under 20 students. I first provide some context and background; then, we closely analyze prepared readings together in seminar-type discussions. Every meeting is very much a two-way street, mutually challenging and enriching. The students in their reactions to the material raise in acute terms the question of why we care about any works of art, literature, or history; how and why they speak to us across time and space; how widely their reception varies, and how important it is for these different receptions to be voiced and heard. Haywood Gandy's final paper (written in August 2015) offers an example of how students' lived experiences and insights inform past reflections with their own perspectives, as they take ancient conversations in new directions and blend ancient voices with their own:

> Cicero said, "To be ignorant of what occurred before you were born is always to remain a child." I wonder, are we a fully grown society, in that we know what happened in our past? The government of the few has been tried and failed not only in ancient Athens but in our own recent history. What was an entire society that was built on and by slave labor? Was this democracy? We have an entire history to examine and learn from ... If we decide to grow up in the way Cicero suggests and learn from our past, we can be greater than we imagine.

In the case of Greek tragedy, the students closely analyze the texts as in any other classroom: the poetry, context, political significance, and so on. Yet at any given time, we are doing much more than "just" literary criticism or historical analysis. Their mode of engaging the works is raw and direct. This is neither sheerly an intellectual exercise for its own sake, nor a detached analysis of ancient poetry as art or testimony of a distant past. It is never just a play or a plotline that we are discussing; these myths are often deeply reminiscent of these men's lives: their own, their peers', and their families'.[8]

What makes the ancient myths especially appealing, according to the students, is the ambiguity of their heroic figures. Greek plays portray humanity in all of its manifestations. In them, we see human life in all its chaos. The characters present a window for looking at and exploring what it means to be human that is particularly rich because it is deeply nuanced and multi-faceted. The plays open up questions about the potential in each of us for a wide range of decisions and outcomes, and the many forces at work both within and without us that lead to these outcomes. Those who one moment excel, and channel that excellence into glorious achievements, can in the next unwittingly destroy their loved ones, or themselves. They are flawed human beings whose actions are provoked by a wide range of factors (including the gods), who hesitate, doubt, destroy and regret, and are relatable in their fallibility and vulnerability. We return to Heracles (Euripides') multiple times over the semester: the very same man who performs the 12 Labors, destroys monsters, and saves so many also annihilates his whole family while possessed by the vengeful goddess

Hera. What of that possession – what are we to make of those moments in which the ancient Greeks tell us that such and such a hero or heroine committed something while a god impassioned them or struck them with madness? How do we disentangle circumstances from the important notions of individual agency and responsibility? Theseus' words to Heracles to stop him from committing suicide after he kills his wife and children resonate deeply: what of the hero's many other deeds? Should a man be defined by what he does in one moment, or what he does over a lifetime?

At the close of term, I give my students the option of recommending readings to enrich future iterations of the syllabus with comparative materials. I also put the question to them: did they care about our texts, and why? Many respond that the Classics are a crucial example of the Humanities' ability to "give us back our Humanity."[9] This was the expression used by reentering citizen Marquis McCray, who was incarcerated for 27 years, and who has been (and continues to be) one of my main interlocutors and partners for the ongoing series of public-facing events I have been moderating with support from the Whiting Foundation.[10] McCray states,

> "Greek literature does not establish hierarchies and it doesn't moralize everything; it just announces what is. It describes the human heart and the human condition as they are." He adds, "Classical writings are a part of Humanity's ongoing dialogue. A conversation which encompasses all; the good, the bad, and the ugly to be found in the human condition. These stories, albeit entertaining, also inspire and inform. More than this, they nourish, nurture, and encourage … We find within the classical texts not-so-civil or virtuous behaviors demonstrated by the same characters in whom we found inspiration: the Glory-bound Achilles reduced to what is tantamount to the bully that we despise; the sagacious Odysseus so guilefully duplicitous and deceptive that his ethics and morality fall into question. What shock confronts the reader, when it is discovered that the kind, supportive Theseus was responsible for what can only be defined as crimes against humanity? And who does not cringe as they witness the horror that is our mighty Heracles indiscriminately slaughtering women and children? What manner of men are these? In a word, 'common!' Dual in nature, these men are arch-typical of humanity's perfectly imperfect."

When Heracles wants to take his own life, his faithful friend Theseus helps him regain a sense of worth, recalling his past and appealing to his

male pride. In a last-ditch attempt to help him find the courage to
persist, he resorts to a misogynistic slur, calling him "womanish." "Ah,
my favorite passage," I jokingly tell my students. "Don't lack courage =
'don't be womanish'." We laugh. Some are indignant. Most know female courage of Heraclean proportions first-hand. In countless essays
and in class, they mention the crucial role that "strong" women play in
their lives: mothers, sisters, daughters, wives, partners – women on
whose courage, persistence, steadfastness and reliability they can count.
In the spring of 2019, I brought some Rutgers students from my Hero in
Ancient Greece and Rome class to a visit with EJSP's Lifers Group.
These so-called "tours" are offered by the prison to educate criminal
justice majors (and others) about prison life. Someone asked the Lifers:
what is a hero? In a typical undergraduate classroom, when we discuss
the likes of Achilles or Odysseus, these larger-than-life characters'
strength and other superhuman qualities invariably come up. The Lifers
Group had a different answer: heroes, they said, are those who endure
and support others by enduring. Every single man went on to name
someone who accomplished heroic feats for them, albeit in humble,
discrete ways: a mother, sister, aunt, grandmother, daughter who kept
them going and supported them unconditionally through it all, in spite
of extreme hardship and deprivation; someone who persisted in going
through the grind of sometimes thankless, unfulfilling work day after
day, providing emotional and material support with whatever limited
means they had; that day, every single one of them without exception
named a woman.[11] Female heroes were also frequently mentioned by
the men in class. One compared his sister to Tecmessa, the true hero of
Sophocles' *Ajax* in his eyes: she stands by Ajax, convincing his men to
stay and support him right up until the fatal moment when he takes his
own life. She is not the teary weakling some mistakenly claim her to be,
he said; she shows outstanding strength in the face of unfathomable
adversity and loss.

  When reading the *Trojan Women,* undergraduates often react as
some critics have: they see the play as "one long lament" without much
action. Not so for the men in prison. Euripides' enslaved queen
Hecuba and her fellow captives in the *Trojan Women*, who continue to
sing in the midst of dire adversity, resonate in an entirely different and
direct manner, inspiring conversations about loss and the preservation
of identity in the face of isolation and within threatened or destroyed
communities; and about the essential, therapeutic role of song in
preserving a persecuted group's identity and struggles across generations, and in retaining that community's sense of cohesion and dignity

in the face of oppression. "The Trojan women's laments speak to me directly," said a student in our Classical Mythology class. "They are their negro spirituals."[12]

The students' written and spoken reflections stress time and again how these plays speak to them across space and time, in a variety of ways. When our course ended (summer 2015), a "Lifer" wrote,

> The most important thing that I learned is our interconnectedness to the past and ... to each other. There is a transcending element about the human condition. The happiness, pain, and tragedy felt by those yesterday touches us today. This connection knows no boundaries and has no limits; it cares nothing about race or gender.

The works provide a framework for reflecting on what it means to be human and how we might go about understanding ourselves and each other. When I ask what the Classics mean to him, McCray calls them an essential part of "Humanity's conversation." In the same breath, he also questions the strange notion of incarceration as "restorative justice": "How can we speak of restorative justice or rehabilitation if there was an imbalance within the society claiming to restore that balance to begin with?" Teaching behind bars (and, in our case, Classics) is but a small cog in the wheel of redressing countless imbalances, not least in individuals' and communities' access to learning and certain forms of content too long the preserve of only the happy few. For Humanity's conversation to be complete, the reception of that content by all – and the voicing of that reception – also must be heard and amplified.

Engaging with the Humanities brings us all back to our shared Humanity. This has been the premise and basis for the Whiting foundation grant project I have been implementing this year, titled "The public face of emotions: public engagement, prison and the emotions in our lives": a series of public-facing performances and conversations with formerly incarcerated persons. Together with the broader public, we watch an excerpt of Greek drama performed live by theater actors, before conversing about the play's relevance and significance to them, as mass incarceration survivors. Each session centers on specific emotions, such as shame, fear, anger, hope, compassion, grief, and friendship. So far, we have held several events so far, at Rikers Island, the New York Society for Ethical Culture (NYSEC), the Players Club of NYC, Howard University, the Middlesex County Community ReEntry Coalition, and the Philadelphia Ethical Society.[13] Our most recent event focused on compassion, reentry, and Sophocles' *Philoctetes*, and took the form of an interview with an interview with Chris Hedges for his show, On Contact.[14] Further sessions are forthcoming.[15]

My project harnesses the power of Greek drama and epic to help us understand human lives and emotions through storytelling. The ancient plays serve as a window onto the human heart and an opening for each of us to recognize the universal traits we all share. Building on these works' ability to spark conversation and transformative engagement between diverse audiences about what defines us as human beings, my current work aims to provide a platform for the voices of the formerly incarcerated to be heard. These events provide a chance for all to engage in communal conversations that help build civic bridges by raising concepts essential to the healing and greater cohesion of our communities: human dignity, justice, and resilience. Our conversations address systemic structural, legal and social issues directly and indirectly, by way of the poetic works of Sophocles and Euripides. Ancient storytelling connects us to modern lives. Invariably and seamlessly, as we examine the ancient works, we are led to discuss their relevance to life before, during, and after prison. We take on the critical issue of mass incarceration from a novel angle, by presenting a counter-narrative to punitive criminal justice, putting the shared humanity of all front and center.

An important premise for our discussions involves Aristotle's questioning of the dichotomy between emotion and reason. Shedding light on the cognitive component of the emotions helps us recognize their legitimate basis, while also inviting us to consider the range of possible outcomes and actions taken in response to them.[16] Heracles kills his family in a bout of madness; yet often it is not madness but pain, fear, anger, or grief that make the men and women of these ancient plays act as they do. McCray draws parallels between these figures – Achilles, Heracles, Ajax and Medea – and the mind frame he says was his as an adolescent growing up in Newark: "a lack of choice combined with a lack of sense of humanity, and just a lot of anger." Thus, we ask: can anger ever be a justified and righteous form of indignation and hence closely linked to Justice?[17] What happens if the basis for that anger is denied recognition? Nafeesah Goldsmith, a reentering citizen and social justice advocate who has been a regular speaker at my Whiting events, uses Medea's story to highlight the stigma and prejudices associated with the "angry woman" stereotype and incarcerated women, as well as the considerable damage that these preconceived notions wreak on the women.[18]

Another set of emotions central to our discussions are those of hope and compassion. In Euripides' *Hecuba,* the eponymous queen suffers an unfathomable betrayal from a trusted friend on top of devastating grief at the loss of her children, and becomes bent on destruction and revenge at any cost; in the *Trojan Women,* by contrast, both she and Andromache try to find hope in the face of utter destruction and despair, enslavement and total loss. What kept these men and women behind bars going when all seemed lost, and they faced decades-long sentences? *Hope ... and anger. Overwhelming grief.* Theseus provides Heracles with a sense of worth and the will to carry on. I ask: who was *your* Theseus? *An older peer behind bars who provided friendship or hope, sometimes without a single word exchanged, say, in the form of a pair of shoes and a book left in their younger counterpart's cell.* The figure of Philoctetes and the mental and physical pain caused by his isolation lead us to discuss solitary confinement, which nearly all of my students who have "maxed out" (i.e., served their full sentence) faced at one time or another, sometimes for several consecutive years. But the pain of isolation continues after their release. Philoctetes echoes the pain of reentry for these men and women – social, financial, psychological and physiological pain, to be sure, but a deeper pain as well, stemming from another form of isolation: the separation from comrades who stayed behind bars, and the feeling of ineffable loss and guilt that comes with leaving them behind.[19]

In *Teaching to Transgress,* bell hooks writes: "The classroom, with all its limitations, remains a location of possibility ... in <which> we have the opportunity to labor for freedom, to ... face reality even as we collectively imagine ways to move beyond boundaries, to transgress.[20] This is education as the practice of freedom." Hooks' words ring especially true in the case of education behind bars. The metaphor of education as a means of moving "beyond boundaries" is a powerful reminder of the very real physical boundaries that surround our students, and the place of education in providing them the means to surmount them.

Notes

1 See https://www.whiting.org/scholars/public-engagement-programs/seed-grant and Matt Butler's Just One Foundation: http://j1foundation.org/. I also received support from the Society for Classical Studies' Classics Everywhere grant; see https://classicalstudies.org/scs-blog/nina-papathanasopoulou/blog-can-studying-classics-encourage-empathy-and-equity. Actors included members of the Resident Acting Company, as well as Tabatha Gayle and Martin Lewis.

2 Demenkoff is Director of Arts Education for the NYC Department of Corrections' Programs & Community Partnerships in Fine and Performing arts.

3 Both spoke at the Aperture Foundation, at an event curated by Rutgers professor Nicole Fleetwood: https://aperture.org/blog/fleetwood-prison-portraits/.

4 For example, Soph. *Trach.* 1278. Contrast human characters, who watch their agency play out and suffer as a result (Allen-Hornblower 2016).

5 https://news.rutgers.edu/feature/flip-wilson-memorial-scholarship-opens-new-horizons-rutgers-student/20150629#.Xe1yCpNKhqw. Mountainview began as a small, independent operation within Rutgers University, founded by professor Donald Roden: https://news.rutgers.edu/news/rutgers-expands-opportunities-former-inmates/20150913#.Xfvp-JNKhox.

6 NJ-STEP initially offered Associate's degrees (AA); it now includes a BA program as well. I taught a BA class at EJSP on Transgression in Ancient Greek Society and Culture and Beyond in the fall of 2019.

7 A recent graduate at EJSP, Lavonta Bass, delayed an early release from prison so his son could see him graduate and deliver the valedictorian oration: https://www.cbsnews.com/news/college-prison-graduates-new-jersey-say-degrees-help-them-transcend-prisons-walls-nj-step-2019-12-20/.

8 On the challenges that come with the potential triggers in myths, see Padilla Peralta in this volume.

9 These are McCray's words; see more about him and their significance below, pp. 17–18. See also Allen-Hornblower and McCray 2021; and Allen-Hornblower, Goldsmith, and McCray 2021.

10 For more on the project, see above, n. 1 and below, pp. 17–19.

11 I have not (yet) been assigned to teach in the NJ women's prison for geographical reasons. Regarding the disparities in support for men and women behind bars, see below, p. 18 and Allen-Hornblower, Goldsmith, and McCray 2021.

12 I have withheld the names of students still on the inside due to DOC regulations.

13 For the Philadelphia Ethical Society event, "Rediscovering Our Humanity: Reading the Classics Behind Bars and Beyond," including performances of excerpts of Euripides' *Medea* and Sophocles' *Philoctetes*, see Allen-Hornblower, Goldsmith, and McCray 2021.

14 McCray and I discussed Sophocles' *Philoctetes* and what it can tell us about the damage wrought by mass incarceration. See Allen-Hornblower and McCray 2021.

15 I am preparing the publication of a monograph partly based on our Whiting events.

16 On cognition and emotion in Aristotle, see especially Fortenbaugh 1975; Konstan 2006.

17 On anger, Justice, and the legacy of Audre Lorde: https://www.blackpast.org/african-american-history/speeches-african-american-history/1981-audre-lorde-uses-anger-women-responding-racism/; regarding anger and the BLM movement see, e.g., https://berkleycenter.georgetown.edu/responses/righteous-anger-black-lives-matter-and-the-legacy-of-king.

18 Women generally receive less external support as a result of this stigma and prejudice, with sometimes devastating consequences for their mental health—and their families. See Allen-Hornblower, Goldsmith, and McCray. 2021.

19 For more on this matter, see the discussions referenced in nn. 13 and 14.

20 hooks 1994, 207.

Works cited

Allen-Hornblower, E. 2016. *From Agent to Spectator: Witnessing the Aftermath in Ancient Greek Epic and Tragedy*. Trends in Classics—Supplementary Volumes, 30. Berlin, Boston: De Gruyter.

Allen-Hornblower, Emily, and Marquis McCray. 2021. "The Power of Classics." Interview by Chris Hedges. *On Contact*, February 20, 2021. Video, 26:59. https://www.youtube.com/watch?v=r1AmlxnweFE

Allen-Hornblower, Emily, Nafeesah Goldsmith, and Marquis McCray. 2021. "Rediscovering Our Humanity: Reading the Classics Behind Bars and Beyond." Filmed January 2021 by the Philadelphia Ethical Society. Video, 1:25:01. https://www.youtube.com/watch?v=oNMucB3YxiQ&feature=youtu.be

Fortenbaugh, W. 1975. *Aristotle on Emotion*. London: Duckworth.

Gandy IV, Haywood S. 2015. "Ancient Civilizations, modern democracies: Forgotten Lessons." Final paper submitted for History 101 course at Northern State Prison.

hooks, b. 1994. *Teaching to Transgress: Education as the Practice of Freedom*. New York: Routledge.

Konstan, D. 2006. *The Emotions of the Ancient Greeks*. Toronto, CA: University of Toronto Press.

2 "Because we've done bad things": understanding *timē* in prison

Elizabeth Bobrick

When I talk about teaching classical mythology and literature in a maximum-security prison, people tend to ask me the same questions: "Aren't you afraid?" and "Can they really do college-level work?" I'm practiced in giving short or long answers to both, depending on the audience, but most people want to hear all I can tell them. The one question that caught me off guard, and that I didn't know how to answer, came from one of my students. He said, "Do people think we can't do this work because we've done bad things?" There was no bitterness or sarcasm in his voice; he just wanted to know. The moment stays with me, and I'll return to his question.

As for the first question: no, I was never afraid. I knew from the outset that I wouldn't be wandering through the cellblocks, as some people imagine when they hear the words "prison education." After going through a TSA-style search at the front desk, with officers searching our bags for contraband, and then being escorted through as many as nine locked gates, I found the conventionality of the classroom unexpectedly comforting: linoleum tile floor, painted cinderblock walls, chair desks for the students, a big desk for me, a whiteboard, and a projector.

Still, I never forgot that we were in a high-security prison. During our three-hour classes, corrections officers patrol the corridor, watching us through the window that makes up most of one wall. The men are not allowed to come to class with pens or pencils; we have to pass them out and then collect them at the end of class, and lock them in a file cabinet. (We were supposed to count them, but I never did.) Once, my flash drive fell on the floor, and I didn't notice. I was lucky that a colleague found it when he came in to teach. If it had ended up in a student's possession, the warden could have shut down our entire program.

All the ways we are used to communicating with our campus students – email, class message boards, file sharing – are impossible.

We have to distribute everything they need well ahead of time. When the facility goes under lockdown unannounced, which happens at least once a semester, we must quickly revise our syllabus, and then spend precious time in the next class reviewing it and reassuring the students. Any unexpected change makes them anxious. Our courses provide much needed stability as well as intellectual stimulation. So, am I afraid? No. Do I find the circumstances vexing, and do I always need to maintain a calm exterior for the students' sake? Yes.

The question "Aren't you afraid?" is, I suspect, a way of asking if I'm afraid of the men themselves. I'm not. Over six years I've taught roughly 50 men in the same maximum-security prison; only two ever raised their voices to me. In each case, they were more frustrated and anxious than angry, and apologized later; the other students murmured reassurances and thanks to me as they filed out.

Now to the second question: Can our incarcerated students really handle the same courses we offer on campus? Can they understand and write about Greek epic and tragedy as well as the undergrads I am used to teaching at an elite institution?[1]

Until I taught my first class, I wasn't sure that they could. I knew that the admissions process was lengthy and competitive. Prospective students must have a clean disciplinary record and the warden's permission to apply. The initial pool of applicants goes through several rounds of interviews with program administrators and university faculty. Those approved to move forward write short essays in response to prompts designed to demonstrate critical thinking skills. After a final round of interviews, approximately 15 students are accepted, a fraction of those who apply.

The essential difference between the campus and incarcerated students is demographic. With very few exceptions – and those exceptions, not surprisingly, were almost all white men – the prison students had grown up within what Paul Farmer (2004) has called "structural violence." Connecticut is the wealthiest state in the nation, but its largest cities are blighted by poverty, underfunded schools, high crime rates, and, of course, systemic racism. Many of my students had been incarcerated since they were teenagers. What could I expect from the students, given what I knew about their home communities?

Once in class, I found out that one of my assumptions was accurate: many of my students struggled with organizing their ideas in written exams, not because of some innate inability, but because they had no training. I taught several of the same students three years apart, and saw how much they had improved with experience – so much so that they were now helping newer students. Nevertheless, many of them were already good writers, and all of them read with an attention to detail that I seldom see among my campus students. The stories of ancient Greek mythology, however, were unfamiliar to even the most highly self-educated men in class. By contrast, most of our traditional students come into class knowing a little about the Greek pantheon. I thought that might be an obstacle to my incarcerated students' comprehension, but I was wrong.

Our traditional students may have read *Antigone* or *Oedipus the King* in high school, but those plays, with their clashing rocks of fate and character, show little of the capricious nature of the gods' cruelty and favoritism. I have to keep reminding them that these gods are not good, or even incidentally interested in doing good. In story after story, deities punish mortals guilty of infractions against them, and, as often as not, go on to wipe out their whole families and communities. Even if an offense is unwitting or accidental, the gods will have their way. They also fight with each other, when one tries to usurp the powers of another, or harm their worshippers. Their overwhelming concern is protecting their privileges and honors.

As I've written elsewhere, my incarcerated students, like their on-campus counterparts, were dismayed that the gods punished innocents, and were equally horrified by human intrafamilial murders (Bobrick 2014). "What is *wrong* with these people?" one of them asked, after yet another member of the House of Atreus killed an immediate family member. I'd assumed that they'd be at least as puzzled about the gods' behavior as were the students on campus, but the topic didn't dominate conversation. I wondered why.

At the end of the semester, I posed the question to one of my students, a man of deep Christian faith. We spoke in the prison version of office hours: desks together in a corner of the classroom, talking in low voices. "Weren't you surprised by these gods?" I asked. He chuckled. "If you've grown up as a Black man in America, you're not surprised by these gods."

The stories of the gods doing what they wished and mortals suffering what they must described a pattern of domination and resistance with which the men were familiar. It had shaped their lives before incarceration, and it persisted – with different players in the positions of power – behind the high walls topped with razor wire. Even so, I hadn't expected them to find as much relevance to their lives in *the Homeric Hymn to Demeter*, but they did, particularly when it came to Demeter's loss and recovery of her *timē*, a concept that my campus students initially find difficult to grasp fully. No one-word equivalent conveys the inseparable combination of status, material goods and control of territory, or the importance of *timē* as a tool of social organization.

To quickly summarize *HHD*: When Zeus allotted honors and territories to the gods after his rise to power, Demeter received control over the earth and its bounty. Hades was made king of the Underworld. They were equals – or so Demeter thought – but Zeus permitted Hades to kidnap their daughter Persephone and take her into the realm of the dead. Demeter finds herself without allies. In sorrow, she leaves Olympus to live among mortals and become nursemaid to a human child. Her attempt to make him immortal is misunderstood by his terrified mother, who stops her. In a rage, Demeter sheds her disguise, and ceases living among humans. Although the child's royal family and city atone for the inadvertent insult by building a temple and conducting yearly rites in Demeter's honor, the incident rekindles her divine rage. She takes up her full powers as a goddess again, and suspends the world in perpetual winter. Without the crops, humans starve, and so cannot offer sacrifices, thereby depriving the gods of their rightful *timai*. This is too much for Zeus. He grants more honors to Demeter, and orders Hades to restore Persephone to her mother. Even so, Hades manages to keep her for six months of every year.

In my introductory lecture, I explained the cultural context of the poem, just as I do with my campus undergraduates: *HHD*'s importance as an aetiological myth; its reflection of actual marriage rites and their association with funerals; its singularity as a myth that emphasizes a loving bond between mother and daughter; and its uniqueness as a story of female resistance to patriarchal power. I presented it as an account of a war begun by the violation of *timē* and a peace brought about by its restoration.

I assumed that my incarcerated students would have as much difficulty understanding *timē* as do my campus students. I was wrong. For them, respect – understood as deference, with or without admiration – is fully equivalent to *timē*: an allotment of privileges, material goods, and widely recognized status ensuring the safety of one's family and possessions. Sociologist Elijah Anderson observes that "respect" in urban communities functions as a force of social organization "whose caveat is vengeance, or payback" (Anderson 1999, 67). Material goods – expensive clothing, jewelry, and guns – play a role in signaling that an individual must be respected (Anderson 1999, 72–76). One way to assert status is to take the possessions of others.[2] Disrespect can take the form of encroaching on the territory of a rival drug dealer, or it can result from what seems to be minor conflict between individuals. For example, an accidental collision between two students in a high school corridor, if taken as a form of disrespect, can escalate quickly and end in lethal violence (Barber 2019, 186–87).[3] The important role that violent behavior can acquire is aptly conveyed by something one of my students wrote in a different context: "Before coming into prison I did not explicitly think about violence. I lived in it … Violence became not only a medium of communication and security, it became social capital. If you were unwilling to exercise violence, especially to defend yourself, you would be ostracized: a social outcast among social outcasts."

My students were surprised and pleased to learn that an ancient Greek concept conveyed the complexity of social dynamics in which displays of respect and disrespect were literally matters of life and death.[4] One student told me that *timē* gained such currency that even men outside the program were using it in conversation: "I heard it in the yard."[5] *HHD* spoke to the men beyond its theme of conflict generated by Zeus' and Hades' disrespect for Demeter. For them, it was not a story with a happy ending, with justice served and everyone better off than they were before. As they saw it, Demeter accepted her compensation because she had to; otherwise, she would never see her daughter again. It was a story of reconciliation, yes, but one that began with an unprovoked violation of a compact. Demeter never got full restitution; she got compensation. What Zeus and Hades did, before and after Penelope's abduction, only confirmed the status quo: the most powerful were free to disobey the rules.

The myth resonated with my students in another way. Many of the men, even very young men, had children whom they could seldom see, and then only briefly. They understood the helplessness of children and how easy it is to lose them, or lose respect in their eyes. When we had our brief one-on-one meetings to review their papers, they would share with pride news of children going to college or graduating from high school. They were also aware of how much their own parents and grandparents suffered because of their incarceration. As one of the men wrote, "Zeus and Hades underestimated a mother's sorrow."[6]

As shocked as they were that Zeus allowed Persephone to be taken from her mother, none of my students expressed any identification with the abducted daughter, probably because she was helpless and female. They noted (with some amusement, as if she were a teenager trying to fool her mother) that she lied to Demeter about having been forced to eat the pomegranate seed Hades gave her.[7]

My experience teaching *HHD* and many other classical texts is not unique. To give one example: a friend who taught an American studies course at the same prison had this to say: "My campus students rarely notice a fact about *The Great Gatsby* that students [at prison] noticed immediately – that Jay Gatsby is a hustler and Nick Carraway a rich kid who enjoys crossing to the other side of the tracks for a while and then congratulates himself on getting back to safety." In other words, conventional academic preparation does not guarantee understanding.

We may laugh at this story – and I did – but we should remember that as academics we cannot so easily shed the perspective we share with many of our traditional students. Obliviousness, intentional or not, is its own form of ignorance. We benefit as teachers and scholars by seeing our discipline through what Johanna Hanink describes as a different "template of reception," one "more concerned with how the ancient past is visibly interwoven in the fabric of the present moment" (Hanink 2017). Feminist, queer, and post-colonial studies have allowed us to read ancient texts through a different "template of reception," that is, through the eyes of those historically marginalized. American-style incarceration is a singular form of social exclusion: the incarcerated are largely invisible, and on the rare occasions when they are permitted to speak publicly, we hear only what they have been allowed to say.

When we bring classical texts into prison classrooms, we have a unique opportunity to learn from our students' reception. To give one example of many: when we read the *Bacchae*, they felt no sympathy for Pentheus. He'd insulted his own grandfather, an elder who deserved only respect. Cadmus was more important in their eyes than he had ever been in mine. They were incensed that Dionysus punished him. "What did he do? He tried!" Indeed, what did he do, except be grandfather to a young hothead obsessed with respect?

The incarcerated students' response to the *Bacchae* brings me back to the question, "Can they do the same work as campus students?" Any answer must include **all** the work, not just reading and writing, but disagreeing and persuading. I was not sure when I began teaching in prison if the men would be able to do so in an environment of antagonism and oppression. The corrections officer who gave my colleagues and me our orientation told us to be prepared for a show of explosive tempers. "They throw the desks at each other," he said. I was quite sure that nobody in our program would be throwing desks, but I didn't know if losing an argument would mean losing face.

As it turned out, I found that they disagreed energetically, but without anger, and they were open to being persuaded by a contrary view. As one student explained to a group of university trustees visiting our class, "I used to think that if anyone disagreed with me, he was my enemy. We were never going to talk again. Now I know that it doesn't have to be like that. We can listen to each other." A Black student added that he no longer followed the racial self-segregation customary in prisons; "Now that brother and I talk all the time," he said, pointing to a white student who lived on his cellblock. I was reminded of Danielle Allen's observation that Athenian tragedy "reflects an awareness that the problem of anger can be addressed with words, and with attempts to restore friendships, as well as with exile" (Allen 2003). We'd seen this already when reading Sophocles' *Ajax*, a play the men found especially moving.

Let me return now to that question from a student: "Do people think we can't do this work because we've done bad things?" I was caught off guard by his frankness, his sense of the distance between his past and present. I also felt embarrassed, as if he'd overheard my conversations with colleagues. We often talk about our students, and we wonder how people who had committed serious crimes had become not only some of the best students we'd ever known but also people we had come to care for deeply.

I had to respond to his question, and quickly, because he'd made himself vulnerable by asking it; most of all, I had to be honest, because incarcerated students are especially alert to deception. So I said yes, I thought that some people did think so. He looked downcast, and I felt terrible. To my relief, another student joined in, saying, in effect, that one's level of education was inevitably racialized in America. Communities of poor Black and Brown people tend to produce poorly educated students, and prisons are full of Black and Brown people.

I also said yes because many who would never think of themselves as racist still may reduce this mix of racism, poverty, and crime to a simple formula: being a person of color and having gone to bad schools results in doing "bad things." Even those who recognize that this equation is simplistic may remain skeptical. I've spoken with people in and outside the academy who wonder if we unconsciously inflate the quality of our students' work because we admire their intellect, determination, and enthusiasm. Anyone who teaches the incarcerated must recognize the importance of this question. If our incarcerated students really can do the same work as our campus students, then we sometimes have to let them fail. It's distressing to see the dejection and self-doubt of a student who gets a low grade on an assignment. In the class I've been describing, two men told me that they might quit after I gave them D's on a paper. (They didn't, and are now among the program's strongest students.) We have to be willing to remind them that college is hard. It's supposed to be.

Teaching in prison is hard, too, because it is heartbreaking. Yes, our students are insightful, dedicated, and enthusiastic, and, in my experience, witty and ready to laugh, a quality I particularly enjoy. That said, classrooms behind walls are beacons of light because they exist within darkness. There is an undeniable element of tragedy in prison education, more prosaic than the doomed families and armies of Greek myth, but every bit as grim and unalterable. My colleagues and I often wonder how the students we know ended up here. Why did they "do bad things"? Why didn't they choose a different path? I don't know; I wonder if they know. I've heard them describe their younger selves as "knuckleheads," that is, young men who are always in trouble. I have seldom felt as proud of my campus undergraduates as I have been of my incarcerated students, and I know that my colleagues in other fields and other prison education programs feel the same. Sadly, that pride exists within the uncomfortable truth that we know them *only* because they are in prison.

Incarcerated students often say that being in class makes them feel human again. That sentiment used to make me happy; over time, it has become bittersweet. No one's sense of their own humanity should depend on keeping in good graces with a jailer, or on the social conscience of a university's administration and faculty, or the state's interest in saving money by reducing recidivism.

The pandemic of 2020 shut down our classes in the middle of the spring semester. Soon after, the state's Department of Corrections gave us unprecedented permission to write to our students (as a group, not individually) and they were allowed to write back to us (again, not individually).[8] In my letter, I'd encouraged them to rely on the strength and grit they'd always shown in class. One student, now imprisoned for over 20 years, wrote back,

> I don't feel strong. I feel broken and tired. There are times, many times, when I just want to climb to the highest point in the unit and just yell "I'm tired".... That said, I know I will overcome, despite the grim outlook.

If he can hope, so can I – and I hope he is right.

Notes

1 I've tried to make the distinction between my incarcerated students and the students most of us were trained to teach as clear as I can without over-generalization. I've referred to the latter group as "campus students" or

"traditional students" or "undergraduates" – in other words, usually young people enrolled in two- and four-year colleges. Community college students, however, tend to be far more diverse in age and life experience than their four-year college counterparts. Students in many university and college prison education programs like ours earn credits and are eligible for degrees, so they too are undergraduates, but the prison classroom is their campus.

  I taught the classes I describe here through Wesleyan University's Center for Prison Education. In order to apply for admission to the program, students must have a clean disciplinary record and the warden's approval. The admissions process includes initial interviews with program administrators, the completion of essays that demonstrate critical thinking skills, and another round of interviews with the university's administrators and faculty, not all of whom have taught in prison. Many more students apply than are accepted, in part because classes are limited to 18. Students can be removed from the program at any time at the warden's discretion; instructors are seldom told why.

2 Anderson's foundational work in urban sociology and ethnography has stood the test of time. See, for example, Intravia et al. 2014.

3 Incidents of perceived but unintended disrespect may also set off a chain of violence; once challenged, a response is required. For many such examples, see Barber 2019.

4 Anderson makes clear that the code of behavior governing many of our students' home communities is a response to institutional racism: hopelessness, lack of employment that pays a living wage, inequity of education, and an understandable distrust of law enforcement.

5 The yard is where inmates are allowed to socialize or exercise on a restricted basis. Our students routinely share books and discuss their classes with men not enrolled in the program.

6 When our first cohort of students received their associate's degrees from a local community college, the man they chose to deliver a formal address to the crowd of faculty and dignitaries spoke of his mother's sacrifices and bravery, and the suffering he had caused her.

7 I am sure that our students in our state's prison for women would read the story differently. As I learned in a writing class I taught there, the great majority had been sexually assaulted at a young age. Many were mothers of children who had grown up while they were in prison.

8 Communicating by mail or telephone with our students while they are incarcerated is illegal in my state. I didn't know this the first time I taught, and a few weeks after class was over, I mailed a thank you note directly to a student who'd created a beautiful card for me that all the students signed. I got away with only a stern warning.

Works cited

Allen, Danielle S. 2003. "Punishment in Ancient Athens." In *Athenian Law and Its Democratic Context* (Center for Hellenic Studies On-Line Discussion Series), edited by A. Lanni. Republished with permission in *Demos: Classical Athenian Democracy*, edited by C. Blackwell (Mahoney, A. and

R. Scaife, eds., The Stoa: a consortium for electronic publication in the humanities (www.stoa.org)). http://www.stoa.org/demos/punishment.pdf

Anderson, Elijah. 1999. *The Code of the Street.* New York, London: W.W. Norton.

Barber, Charles. 2019. *Citizen Outlaw: One Man's Journey from Gangleader to Peacekeeper.* New York: Harper Collins.

Bobrick, Elizabeth. 2014. "The Stakes Are High: Tragedy and Transformation Within Prison Walls." *Amphora* 11 (1): 5 and 18–19. https://classicalstudies. org/amphora/stakes-are-high-tragedy-and-transformation-within-prison-walls-elizabeth-bobrick.

Farmer, Paul. 2004. "An Anthropology of Structural Violence." *Current Anthropology* 45 (3): 305–25.

Hanink, Johanna. 2017. "It's Time to Embrace Critical Classical Reception." *Eidolon*, May 1, 2017. https://eidolon.pub/its-time-to-embrace-critical-classical-reception-d3491a40eec3.

Intravia, Jonathan, Kevin T. Wolff, Eric A. Stewart, and Ronald L. Simons. 2014. "Neighborhood-Level Differences in Police Discrimination and Subcultural Violence: A Multilevel Examination of Adopting the Code of the Street," *Journal of Crime and Justice* 37 (1): 42–60.

3 Dialogic pedagogy as a model for teaching classics in prison

Nancy Felson and Nebojša Todorović

Introduction

This chapter is a dialogue between Professor Emerita Nancy Felson and doctoral candidate Nebojša Todorović. Felson taught a semester-long course, "Masculinities in Ancient Greek Literature: from Achilles to Socrates," for the Bard Prison Initiative in the Fall of 2017; Todorović, who taught a beginner's Latin language class for the Yale Prison Education Initiative in the Summer of 2019, is preparing to teach a Classical Civilization course on "Literary Representations of Ancient Masculinities." Although his experience teaching language informs the conversation, we will emphasize the teaching of classical texts in translation and thematically. We first present the theoretical approaches we found useful. Next, we engage in a dialogue about what worked and what was less successful in the Masculinities course on its trial run, also in view of Todorović's forthcoming class.

Pedagogical approaches

Reception Studies has evolved since the 1970s as an approach to literary criticism. Building on the work of Hans-Georg Gadamer and Hans Robert Jauss, among others, it follows the proposition that a text's meaning is realized when its "horizon of expectation" meets that of the reader (Gadamer 1975, 366; Jauss 1982). In other words, meaning is never inherent, always constructed, to be drawn out as part of the historical nature of understanding. It does not exist in an epistemological and historical vacuum but is realized through dialogue at its point of reception. The transformation of "the dead trace of meaning [...] back into living experience" always unfolds within history, as a "fusion of horizons" between past and present, text and reader (Martindale 1993, 7).

In recent years a growing number of Classicists have endorsed the principles of Reception Studies and applied them to widely diverse receptions of ancient Greek and Latin texts.[1] These scholars argue that a dialogue arises from the juxtaposition between ancient texts and more recent interpretations and adaptations. As Julia Gaisser puts it, classical texts are "not teflon-coated baseballs hurling through time [...] until they reach our enlightened grasp; rather, they are pliable and sticky artifacts gripped, molded, and stamped with new meaning by every generation of readers, and they come to us irreversibly altered by their experience" (Gaisser 2002, 387).

This development has implications for our teaching of Classics within the prison system. It is in harmony with the theory and practice of dialogic pedagogy, an approach pioneered by the philosopher and educator Paolo Freire while working in Brazil, Chile, and Bolivia. In designing a pedagogy for the oppressed people of colonized nations, Freire rejected practices that reduce educating to a mere "act of depositing" knowledge, in what he calls a "banking model," which he characterizes as an instrument of colonial repression whose goal is to preclude the possibility of dissent. Freire (2005, 72) writes:

> Knowledge emerges only through invention and re-invention, through the restless, impatient, continuing, hopeful inquiry human beings pursue in the world, with the world, and with each other. In the banking concept of education, knowledge is a gift bestowed by those who consider themselves knowledgeable upon those whom they consider to know nothing. Projecting an absolute ignorance onto others, a characteristic of the ideology of oppression, negates education and knowledge as processes of inquiry. The teacher presents himself to his students as their necessary opposite; by considering their ignorance absolute, he justifies his own existence. The students, alienated like the slave in the Hegelian dialectic, accept their ignorance as justifying the teachers' existence—but, unlike the slave, they never discover that they educate the teacher.

Conversely, according to Freire (2005, 115), participants in dialogic pedagogy make explicit their "real consciousness" of the world, broadening their perceptual horizons. For them and for their teachers, drawing on their "background awareness" allows them to become more human. Dialogic teachers are not mere facilitators: they do not fully relinquish a position of leadership in the classroom, downplaying their expertise. Instead, they "stimulate learners to live a critically conscious presence in the pedagogical and historical process." Teachers and students share their resources and experiences.

While the banking model is congruent with conservative strands in Classics scholarship that venerate "the classical tradition" and emphasize the supposed timelessness of ancient texts, the dialogic model is closer in spirit to creative feminist, LGBQT, and classical reception reading strategies that value multiple perspectives.

In Felson's class, dialogic engagement took various shapes. For example, students brought their notions of masculine competition, conflict, violence, and cross-generational solidarity into the early discussions, articulating and fine-tuning these notions as they moved through the texts. The memory of what had led to their incarceration, the anguish of separation from their families, and the anxiety about reunions (*nostoi*) enriched the conversations. Rather than regarding their experiences as extraneous to the worldview of the Homeric poems, Felson welcomed the students' input as they developed their individual, personal understandings. Together, they generated a typology of family structures: two-parent families with a domineering vs a gentle, inclusive father; single parent families (male or female) with an absent heroic father or absent dead father or absent (divine) mother, etc. Felson provided sets of guiding questions and a Homeric Greek vocabulary list. They examined Telemachus' development to manhood as a son deprived of his father from infancy, who lacks any beneficial mentoring for the first 20 years of his life – a son who knows of his father only through hearsay and whose male role models are his mother's 108 suitors, paradigms of dependency and unrealized manhood who are only slightly older than himself. The class compared Telemachus' maturation in the *Odyssey* to that of Achilles in the *Iliad*, and, among the Olympians, of Apollo in the *Homeric Hymn to Apollo*, and Zeus and Cronus in Hesiod's *Theogony*. Turning to Greek tragedy, they continued to extract an evolving set of patterns from the varied interactions between fathers and sons.

Sophocles' *Philoctetes* introduced another complicated father-son relationship. It also illuminated a key function of the dialogic teacher's mission: to help the students internalize these texts. Felson guided the discussion of the impact on Neoptolemus of Achilles' long absence, his heroism, and his recent death on the battlefield. Why was the youth so susceptible to Odysseus' manipulations? The mentoring of Neoptolemus was of special interest to the incarcerated students, who empathized with the fatherless youth.

The class also staged scenes from Aristophanes' *Clouds* through a "Reacting-to-the-Past" strategy that focused on the character of

Socrates. Rather than imposing "authoritative" themes and messages of Aristophanes' play onto the classroom, Felson asked the students to perform key passages from the play. One student volunteered to play Socrates and to coordinate the roles of Strepsiades (the indebted, cantankerous father), Pheidippides (the rebellious son), and Good and Bad Argument. After the performance, the class discussed the kind of pedagogy in Aristophanes' comedy. What notion of education did the play's lead characters attribute to Socrates' fictional school, the Thinkery? What did the father expect his son to gain from attending? How did that backfire? And why did the father himself then enroll? The class left open the question of what the comic playwright *meant* by his negative (and hilarious) portrayal of Socrates and Socratic education. The students were asked to contrast the Thinkery with their expectations for their Masculinity course and its philosophy. They were introduced to Freire's ideas of "banking" and "dialogic" pedagogy, and they reflected on the pedagogy that would best serve their own learning styles and goals.

Toward the end of the semester, the class examined the character of Socrates in Athens circa 399 BCE. At the University of Georgia, Felson had regularly taught "Reacting to the Past – Athens 403 BCE," a citizenship game about the restoration of the Athenian democracy after the defeat by Sparta in the Peloponnesian War.[3] She brought this experience to the Masculinity classroom through a session dedicated to the trial of Socrates. Felson divided the 12 students into prosecutors, defenders, and a jury, and instructed them to use the Socratic techniques of *elenchus*, embedded dialogues, mythical allusions, and analogy in their prepared speeches, and to support their arguments by quoting from C.D.C. Reeves' *Trial of Socrates* with texts from Aristophanes, Xenophon, and Plato. The students could use notecards but had to deliver their speeches extemporaneously. They developed criteria for assessing Socrates' life and worthiness as an Athenian citizen. Then, as Athenian citizens, they debated. The jury, using pebbles (as in the *dikastērion* of ancient Athens) to indicate their judgment about Socrates, decided to acquit the philosopher of both charges. Such moments of participatory pedagogy embody Freire's desire to replace the condescending notion that educators are "civilizing the natives" with the idea that pedagogy is a humanizing venture for both teachers and students, where "being human" is a process that requires constant vigilance.

In the following conversation, we reflect on what was distinctive about the students' receptions of the *Iliad*, the *Odyssey*, *Philoctetes*, *Clouds*, and three Platonic dialogues. We also consider what should be changed in future courses so as to enhance student participation and fortify their self-knowledge as they read ancient texts and learn from one another. The Bard Prison Initiative provides a safe space for easy exchange of ideas and experiences — as a "third space" between inside and outside.[2]

A dialogue

Nebo: Let's start with masculinities. Why plural? Does it just relate to the ancient world or does it reflect a multiplicity of masculinities in the prison setting and the classroom in which you taught?

Nancy: I used the plural because there was no uniform pattern for what an adult Greek male was supposed to be, though religious rituals honoring Apollo and Artemis guided Greek youths through a series of age grades on their path to adult manhood and womanhood. In Athens of the classical period, there was more regulation of this journey, especially for young men. The citizen body attempted to codify a uniform notion of the adult male citizen, who would actively participate in the *polis*, head the household, and fight in the frequent wars. However, such regularity is not attested across Greece, in its islands and colonies, in the preceding archaic periods. The multiplicity of patterns made it possible for the students to rethink their own experiences and choices.

Coming of age was a particularly resonant theme for our class. Some had committed crimes in their youth; others had children for whom they were absent fathers; still others had experienced bad mentoring. We examined intergenerational interactions in both epics and discussed efforts by elders to guide (and control) the actions of young men such as Achilles and Telemachus. The students noted the conventional wisdom of the heroic code, that a boy must become a speaker of words and a doer of deeds and must ultimately walk in his father's footsteps. In reading the *Iliad*, we examined Achilles' status as an outsider who critiqued the overarching heroic code. We asked whether such an all-encompassing code served all male characters equally. The students were particularly interested in exploring the causes for and consequences of youths having gone astray. Achilles' reluctance to fit into the adult patterns being thrust upon him raised questions about the very structure of his society and the very values others were urging him to uphold.

So, the *Iliad* gave us an alternative model to the heroic code, one which reflects upon, critiques, and even deconstructs it. In Book 24, Priam relates to Achilles as a father to a son, with respect and warmth, and Achilles responds in kind. They weep together. They break bread. They bond despite their enmity. Similarly, in the *Odyssey*, Odysseus takes the first steps in bonding with his son. He yields his seat to him in the swineherd's hut and includes him in planning the slaughter. In response, at the Bow Contest, Telemachus obeys his father's nod and refrains from stringing the bow. What could have been competition, even enmity, becomes camaraderie. Such models from Homeric epic became the bedrock for our course.

Nebo: The notion of evolving and multifaceted masculinities must have resonated with students' experiences. When I taught Introductory Latin with YPEI, I remember that one of my students showed expertise concerning English vocabulary about sea life (words like *nauta, ae, navis, is, navigo, as* appeared early in our textbook); later, he told me that he was a marine in the first Gulf War, and I remember thinking that going from celebrated veteran to maximum security prison inmate is comparable to Philoctetes' life trajectory. Sophocles' *Philoctetes* is a play that encapsulates your idea of plural masculinities. How did your students react to the play? What was the importance of their personal experiences in reading and interpreting it?

Nancy: When we read the *Philoctetes* and the *Ajax*, the students were startled by Sophocles' innovative representations of the character of Odysseus. In the *Philoctetes*, the playwright casts the Homeric hero as an opportunist, an unloving, ungentle mentor to Achilles' fatherless son, Neoptolemus. Odysseus' misguidance of the susceptible youth appalled them. One student wrote an excellent essay contrasting the rapport between Odysseus and Telemachus in the *Odyssey* with the tension between Odysseus and Neoptolemus in Sophocles' play. The suggestion that Homer's Odysseus had degenerated into a slimy character on the Athenian stage and succumbed to non-heroic values intrigued them. ("He doesn't walk the talk," one student observed.) Nearly all of them admired Philoctetes' moral values, but they also saw the wounded hero as isolated, stubborn, and proud. Their main focus was on the need of the young Neoptolemus for wholesome mentoring. Their conversation kept returning to the idea of surrogate fathers, with a few of them regretting that they had lacked paternal support as young adults. Reading the *Philoctetes* and the *Ajax* prompted them to enrich the typology of fathers that we put on the blackboard class after class.

Nebo: Your comments remind me of the conversations we had about the role of personal experience, of the "baggage" that each student brings to class and to a text. Your interest in the theme of masculinities stems from your family history, right? How can we theorize the role of personal experience in the prison classroom?

Nancy: Yes, I have four brothers and my father was a larger-than-life personality. This is something that prompted my fascination with masculinity. I watched them compete in sports and intellectual matters and saw the impact on my brothers of a very eminent yet caring father, and I remembered times when my brothers (and I) would feel overshadowed. We all avoided our father's field (medicine) and perhaps would have thrived more without having to contend with such a public parent. I shared this with my students, not only as a way to expand the father/son typology that we were developing but to model the sharing of a personal, experiential perspective.

Nebo: The reason I ask about your own family is that we are trying to tease out the unique intuitions of our prison students as they confront new texts. Your students, because of their confinement and the life experiences that led them to being incarcerated, seem to have had a strong reaction to the interconnected themes of bad mentorship, coming of age, and absent, domineering, and surrogate fathers. How did their reactions differ from those of your on-campus students at UGA?

Nancy: In their first set of papers, they wrote about Achilles' rage and impulsiveness. His eventual growth and reflections resonated with them: perhaps they were thinking about their own costly youthful errors in judgment. The passage in *Iliad* 1 in which Athena stays Achilles' hand to prevent his slaying of Agamemnon fascinated them. "Where was Athena when they needed her?" a student asked. Another confessed that he was initially critical of Achilles but felt more empathy once he witnessed the hero's struggles with his own anger. My incarcerated students displayed a deeper level of identification with mythological characters than my students at UGA. This led us to more nuanced interpretations based on a wider range of experiences with rage, violence, and revenge and a deeper sense of the need of a youth for guidance.

By contrast, when I taught Vergil's *Aeneid* to Latin students at Smith College in the 1980s, all three were reluctant to connect emotionally with angry and violent characters. To help them interpret the presence of the Fury at Jupiter's side at the end of the *Aeneid* and Aeneas' decision to avenge Pallas by killing Turnus, I formulated the essay question on the final: "Describe your personal attitudes toward anger and revenge and reflect on how those personal attitudes have shaped your understanding of rage in Book 12 of Vergil's epic." Two students had breakthroughs. In writing their exam, they suddenly realized how dismissive they had been of enraged characters like Juno. They were able to tap into a broader set of emotions as they interpreted the text.

Nebo: When I taught the Latin class, I was surprised by the collective engagement and mutual support. Perhaps because Latin is often associated with class privilege, mastering the language became a point of pride, on an individual and a collective level. In a group of nine "Latinists," the four students who steadily performed at an excellent level in quizzes and exams still regularly attended afternoon study halls in order to support the other students. I remember thinking I should try to recreate this environment of collaborative learning in on-campus language classes. Did you have a similar experience with your on-campus students at UGA? What about your incarcerated students?

Nancy: My students on campus, who were younger and less self-aware than my incarcerated students, tended also to be more attached to their families and less reflective about conflicts. In general, they were unaccustomed to drawing on their personal experiences in interpreting texts. Some of this was a function of age homogeneity in undergraduate classes. In on-campus "Reacting" courses, however, cooperative team spirit was a key motivating factor that enriched the learning experience. Since the Games themselves necessitate such cooperation, even shy or reticent undergrads would become cooperative teammates who delighted in contributing to their team's success.

The life of an incarcerated person is limited by structural constraints. With no access to the Internet and only one shelf dedicated to the Classics in their library (to which they had very limited access), they were unable to do extensive research. This was a significant limitation when they were preparing for the trial of Socrates. At UGA, "Reacting" students would work independently to supplement class materials and discussions; at BPI, this was not possible. Hence the trial was not as satisfying as I had hoped. They needed a deeper knowledge of the political climate in late fifth-century Athens in order to assess whether Socrates was a danger or an asset to the *polis*. They needed to understand what constituted an Athenian citizen. Also, they could not assemble as teams (factions) outside of class to formulate their arguments and challenge one another – another major drawback. In a second run of "Masculinities," I might work up a Trial of Alcibiades, drawing on his biography in Plutarch's *Lives* and using criteria pre-set in classroom discussion. Earlier in the course, we could stage a debate about the morality of Zeus or Prometheus in the *Prometheus Bound*, or about the values of Odysseus in Sophoclean tragedy. Socrates was particularly difficult to put on trial, according to our models, since we know so little of his adolescence: did he even have one?

Nebo: Thank you so much for sharing your experience. Our conversation has helped me re-design my new civilization class. In the spirit of dialogic pedagogy, I plan to keep the title of the class purposely vague and not restrict the topic in terms of period and genre. I was initially thinking along the lines of "Performing Masculinity on the Athenian Stage" or "Sex and Gender in Ancient Rome"; but a less restrictive title would allow me to draw on students' interests and experience. On the first day of class, I will present a draft of the syllabus with a fixed block of key texts (the Homeric poems and selected tragedies) and an overview of central themes. These would include: "The Gods Confront Their Masculinity" (selection from the *Homeric Hymns*, Hesiod's *Theogony*, Callimachus' *Hymns*); "War Literature from Ancient Athens" (poems by Archilochus, Callinus and Tyrtaeus, Aeschylus' *Seven Against Thebes*, excerpts from Herodotus' *Histories*, Aristophanes' *Peace* and *Acharnians*); and "Laughing about Masculinity" (Lysias' *On the Murder of Eratosthenes*, Aristophanes' *Lysistrata* and *Thesmophoriazusae*,

Lucian's *The Mimes of the Courtesans*). Then, with some understanding of how my students conceptualize masculinity, I will dedicate an entire session to finalizing the readings. I will present options for thematic units and invite them to propose others related to our topic. I want to keep the syllabus flexible to allow my students to participate in the development of the class. In that spirit, I will also negotiate with them about what kinds of collective or individual creative assignments would interest them. These could be performances, translations, drawings, songs – anything that would allow them to express the messages of a text in a more personal way, as long as the project could be carried out within the prison setting.

Nancy: Keep in mind the idea that you are not only a mere facilitator but also a teacher hired to share your expertise (an important component of your pedagogy). I'd maintain a balance of power between yourself and your students early in the semester. The art of listening and acknowledging is an essential component of dialogic pedagogy. Low stakes assignments and a welcoming atmosphere in the classroom would gradually build the students' confidence, as in any class. Also, it seems important that you reveal your own interests on the first day of class, so as to validate your own voice in the dialogic exchange. Remember, you are the "teacher" in the sense that you bring to them memorable patterns of behavior and relationships that can help them interpret not only the ancient texts but their own life experiences.

I would, in any case, avoid radically "democratizing the classroom" to the extent that "anything goes." Perhaps, on that first day, you should elicit from your students a set of criteria for evaluating interpretations. You could return to that list, as I did with the typology, and refine it as you and your students moved forward. I like to make a distinction between textual interpretation and creative appropriation. Can we consider the prison classroom to be a site of a variety of receptions, interpretive and creative?

Notes

1 For a thorough discussion about the notion of dialogue in relation to the field of classical reception, see Greenwood 2009, 1–20; Rankine 2006, 3–21; Goff and Simpson 2007, 38–79; Yaari 2018, 1–18.

2 For more on the notion of prison classroom as a third space, see Wilson 2000, 51–66, Novek 2017, 31–51.
3 Reacting to the Past, which consists of elaborate games set at a particular historical period, was invented and pioneered in the 1990s by Mark Carnes, Professor of History at Barnard College. Since then, it has been widely disseminated in the US and abroad. The Athens Game was one of the first to be developed. For information and an overview of this innovative pedagogy, see https://reacting.barnard.edu/about-reacting.

Works cited

Freire, Paulo. 2005. *Pedagogy of the Oppressed*. Translated by Myra Bergman Ramos. New York: Continuum International Publishing Group.

Gadamer, Hans-Georg. 1975. *Truth and Method*. Translated by Joel Weinsheimer, Donald G. Marshall. London: Sheen and Ward.

Gaisser, Julia. 2002. *The Reception of Classical Texts in the Renaissance*. Florence: Olschki Editore.

Goff, Barbara, and Michael Simpson. 2007. *Crossroads in the Black Aegean: Oedipus, Antigone, and Dramas of the African Diaspora*. Oxford: Oxford University Press

Greenwood, Emily. 2009. *Afro-Greeks: Dialogues Between Anglophone Caribbean Literature and Classics in the Twentieth Century*. Oxford: Oxford University Press.

Jauss, Hans Robert. 1982. *Towards an Aesthetic of Reception*. Translated by Timothy Bahti. Minneapolis: University of Minnesota Press.

Martindale, Charles. 1993. *Redeeming the Text: Latin Poetry and the Hermeneutics of Reception*. Cambridge: Cambridge University Press.

Novek, Eleanor M. 2017. "Jail Pedagogies: Teaching and Trust in a Maximum-Security Men's Prison." *Dialogues in Social Justice* 2 (2): 31–51.

Rankine, Patrice D. 2006. *Ulysses in Black: Ralph Ellison, Classicism, and African American Literature*. Madison: The University of Wisconsin Press.

Wilson, Anita. 2000. "There is No Escape from Third Space Theory: Borderland Discourse and the In-Between Literacies of Prisons." In *Situated Literacies: Reading and Writing in Context*, edited by David Barton, Mary Hamilton, Roz Ivanić, 51–66. London: Routledge.

Yaari, Nurit. 2018. *Between Jerusalem and Athens: Israeli Theatre and the Classical Tradition*. Oxford: Oxford University Press.

4 Surmises and surprises: notes on teaching ancient Greek literature in a correctional facility

Amy E. Johnson and Laura M. Slatkin

Thank you. Learning took place. I would of never thought that Ancient Greek mythology could be relevant in today's world, but it very much is.

One of our incarcerated students wrote this comment at the end of a course, and in effect he spoke for all those we taught in this context. Our observations are based on two separate terms of teaching at a NY State Correctional Facility – a medium-security prison for men – roughly 75 miles from New York City. Our first course was on Homer, the second on fifth-century Athenian tragedy. The comments we offer below will, we hope, provide some orientation to others interested in joining this challenging but joyful enterprise.

Our first, enduring surmise proved the most correct and solid: that the literature of ancient Greece, in translation, was both available and relevant to every student. Differences of background and previous education did not seriously impede the impact of this profoundly humanistic material. Our presence and commitment in the classroom as facilitators made this argument, but the literature spoke eloquently for itself. Aeschylus, Sophocles, and Euripides proved no less welcome and resonant than Homeric epic had done in our first course within the prison walls.

A word on the institutional context: our teaching was offered under the auspices of a university program for prison education, through which students can learn an Associate of Arts degree; if they wish, they may, after release, apply to continue on to further coursework in four-year colleges and universities. We came to the program bearing in mind this potential goal, which in a general way aligned with our expectations of teaching undergraduates in a university setting; but we had no knowledge of how the classes would fit into the daily lives of incarcerated people or the daily operations of the correctional facility.

On the day before our first class, we were required to attend an orientation by a volunteer coordinator at the facility. None of it addressed pedagogical or educational concerns, but rather focused on prison protocols and restrictions – for instance, what we couldn't wear or bring into the prison.

We didn't know enough to anticipate that class attendance would be erratic throughout the semester, mostly for reasons over which the students had no control: they would be "called out" of class by the corrections staff (sometimes for medical and counseling matters). We discovered that the rhythm of our presentation of material and assignments needed to take into account, as much as was feasible, that uncertain attendance – and interruptions for "call-outs." The class sessions, moreover, which were scheduled for three hours per week, were often delayed because of prison constraints, so that not infrequently our class time was reduced to an hour and a half.

Since its inception, this program was fortunate in having the support of the Superintendent of the Correctional Facility, who retired in the middle of our second semester and had not yet been replaced by the time we came to the end of it. Yet despite her endorsement of the project and that of the Acting Commissioner of the New York State Department of Corrections, our presence at the facility met with mixed reactions from the corrections officers (prison guards) who were responsible for moving the inmates and us in and out of our designated study areas. On one occasion, when a lockdown the previous evening meant that we had to wait for two hours to be brought to the classroom, we inquired why the prison education program staff had not been alerted to this. It was clear that we were not their top priority.

When we were initially designing our first course, we conferred with a colleague, a political theorist who had taught at the same facility the previous year: did he think the *Iliad* would be of any interest to the students there? He considered, and replied, "Yes, it's about honor." And indeed, our students were quickly responsive to questions of honor and quickly sympathetic to Achilles, reluctant to judge him (as undergraduates so often do) as immature or spoiled and insubordinate. When we read Book 6, the students appreciated the complexity of Hector's decision to rise to the challenge of honorably defending his city, despite the consequences for his wife and child.

But there were surprises. Perhaps the most arresting one came when we had reached Book 22 of the *Iliad*. Hector and Achilles were outside the walls of Troy, and one of the students was reading aloud, a practice we regularly used to highlight passages. His voice broke. Ours would have, too; to both of us this moment in Hector's heroic progress is heartbreaking. But our student went on to chuckle, then laughed out loud – and the majority of the class joined him.

We were dumbfounded, but eventually broke into the merriment to ask the men what was so funny. Hector, they explained, had confidently bragged (in the Book 16 passage we'd read the previous week) that he would defeat Achilles – and here he was, shivering and running. He couldn't live up to his boast. "And he's a coward," they replied with satisfaction. "He's scared." You might pity him, but that didn't mean you wouldn't laugh at him as well.

Here were students whose lives had been lived among other men, threatening and threatened. To claim more than you were capable of delivering, or to run from confrontation, was to risk ridicule. No undergraduate had hinted at such an ethos; at the prison, the whole class seemed to live by it.

What had the earliest audiences of Homeric poetry understood by Hector's flight? Carefully we proceeded through the text:

> They ran by these springs, pursuer and pursued—
> A great man out front, a far greater behind—
> And they ran all out. This was not a race
> For such a prize as athletes compete for,
> An oxhide or animal for sacrifice, but a race
> For the lifeblood of Hector, breaker of horses.
> …
> "I'm not running any more, Achilles.
> Three times around the city was enough.
> I've got my nerve back. It's me or you now.
> But first we should swear a solemn oath.
> With all the gods as witnesses, I swear:
> If Zeus gives me the victory over you,
> I will not dishonor your corpse, only
> Strip the armor and give the body back
> To the Greeks. Promise you'll do the same."
> And Achilles, fixing his eyes on him:
> "Don't try to cut any deals with me, Hector.
> Do lions make peace treaties with men?
> Do wolves and lambs agree to get along?
> No, they hate each other to the core,
> And that's how it is between you and me,
> No talk of agreements until one of us
> Falls and gluts Ares with his blood."
> (*Iliad* 22.178–183 and 277–293, trans. S. Lombardo)

We looked at the comparison of the race to an athletic contest and the contrast of the prizes; by this time, the students were familiar with the spoils of war and Achilles' critique of them. We considered Hector's courage and candor in ultimately facing his opponent and noted his doomed faith that his circumstances were open to negotiation. Finally, we looked at Achilles' terrifying recognition of what mortal combat means.

After this discussion, we showed a brief clip from the movie "Troy." There the scene evolves with no exchange, no verbal reflection. There's a glimpse of the watchers from the wall, but otherwise it might have been a video game: clash and clamor. Our students recognized it as utterly impoverished. Two or three had seen it before and remarked that, having read the poem, they now found it disappointing and misleading.

Brief viewings or readings of intertextual material were an initial guess on our part when assembling the syllabus, and our students responded to them with recognition and enthusiasm, as well as appreciating their variety. Most were of far greater stature than "Troy" – a selection from Tim O'Brien's *The Things They Carried*; battle scenes from the Terrence Malick film "The Thin Red Line," inspired by James Jones's novel of Guadalcanal; a scene from Jean Renoir's "Grand Illusion." These parallels offered Homeric material in forms or idioms more familiar than dactylic hexameter, emphasizing the ongoing resonance of Homeric concerns.

A text that reinforced the connections for our students between the *Iliad* and more contemporary experience was Jonathan Shay's *Achilles in Vietnam*, from which we assigned two chapters. The depth of injury inflicted by a commanding officer's disrespect (or worse) was recognized to cut across historical and cultural differences.

Contemporary analogies seemed less necessary for our discussions of the *Odyssey* than for the *Iliad*. Many of the men in our class spoke of a sense of comradeship that linked easily to the affiliations of comrades-in-arms, to the loyalty that the *Iliad* preeminently values. Every man in our class, however, had a deeply felt affinity with Odysseus. Gods and monsters offered equivalents to the anxieties, hopes, and entanglements that each anticipated or dreaded upon homecoming. And at least half had children who did not know their fathers.

Teaching Greek tragedy (with a different class) brought not only some continuities but also variation. Launching the course (subtitled "Justice, Responsibility, Kinship") with the *Oresteia*, we discovered at the outset that finding a translation that was both accurate and accessible for the students was a more challenging project than we had faced in teaching Homer; and in fact, this was the case with several of the plays we taught. We therefore provided a summary of *Agamemnon*, which seemed too dense with metaphor for an opening selection, and focused on a few individual passages.

The students were especially gripped, and repelled, by Agamemnon's sacrifice of Iphigenia, and were curious to return to it with our final selection of the semester, *Iphigenia at Aulis*. Following this, we were able to have successful, engaged discussions of *Libation Bearers* and *Eumenides*; Orestes' key speech – "What shall I do?" – became a touchstone for our exploration of tragedy with its focus on action and responsibility and its relation to democracy and the claims of the polis.

But another surprise came with *Antigone*. We had the students reading aloud as usual, simply moving around the room during the opening exchange between Antigone and her sister, when one reader – a usually lively participant – balked. "I'm not reading that. I'm not a girl!" We skipped him and eventually talked it out, pointing out the courage and loyalty of Antigone; and we noted that this conflicted classroom incident was strikingly echoed in the action within our subsequent reading, Athol Fugard's *The Island*. In Fugard's play, set in the 1970s apartheid-era South Africa – and specifically in the notorious Robben Island prison where Nelson Mandela was incarcerated for three decades – two cellmates, imprisoned for destroying their passbooks, consider performing a version of Antigone for their fellow prisoners; but one of them objects, as our student did, to playing the part of a woman, believing it will humiliate him, and must be convinced to undertake it.

Beyond this resistance to, as it were, playing the female other, reading *The Island* brought an additional surprise: namely that initially the men displayed only tepid interest in it, although all but one were students of color. We had wrongly surmised that they would know something of the history of modern South Africa. Upon a little questioning, it turned out that no student recognized the word apartheid, although a few had some knowledge of Nelson Mandela. We explained the history of apartheid and passed out a sheet of facts, then noted that Mandela himself had organized a clandestine performance of *Antigone* on Robben Island. Once our students saw what it meant to receive an indefinite sentence for burning your passbook, they became passionate.

More immediately vivid to them was Tanya Barfield's one-act play, *Medallion*, in which an African-American woman confronts a white army general to ask for the Croix de Guerre won by – but never awarded to – her brother, who was killed in battle fighting in the segregated American military in World War I.

Although we had prepared an analytic writing assignment for the coming week, we spontaneously offered them the choice of writing an "extra" scene – perhaps a new conclusion to either *Medallion* or to *The Island*. All but one student seized this opportunity, and the results were remarkable. Not only did the scenes show imagination and creativity, they each took on the idiom, tone, and sensibility of the existing characters. Their writing suddenly demonstrated graceful facility and conveyed real urgency. One of the class made the dead and unhonored brother speak. Another imagined a poignant parting for the two prisoners in *The Island*, one freed on a technicality, the other condemned forever – for the same "crime," as stipulated by pure racism. Before they had taken the material to heart, but this exercise somehow made it especially possible for them to express this, as well as their speculative critical insights. What an argument for offering creative writing classes to incarcerated students!

Among the most absorbing discussions of the semester were those focused on Sophocles' Ajax and, in the following week, on Ellen McLaughlin's *Ajax in Iraq*. First performed in 2008, McLaughlin's play re-imagines Sophocles' tragedy in the context of the contemporary American military as a site for brutality – and betrayal – at the hands of a superior officer. Her work creates a dialogue between ancient and modern that proved especially illuminating for the students; those whose initial response to Ajax had been to assume that the protagonist's suicide was "selfish" toward his family, for example, were helped by the modern play to see that the ancient one rejects that judgment.

The students' enthusiasm for *Ajax in Iraq* led us to another surprise: as they asked us whether there were any film or video versions of McLaughlin's play that they could watch, they made us aware that the majority of them had never seen a play staged. One student said that the only play he had ever seen in his life was one that had been put on in the prison. We had downloaded YouTube material onto USB drives in order to be able to show the class at least some clips from several of our assigned works, including Luis Alfaro's powerful *Oedipus el Rey*, set in the gang culture of south-central LA, and it was evident that watching even brief excerpts of the plays we were reading was both clarifying and invigorating.

Given expressed eagerness from the students, we arranged for a visit from Ellen McLaughlin, who generously agreed to join our final class of the semester to discuss her work with ancient Greek drama and

Ajax in Iraq in particular. Our plan for the last class was to have the students read scenes aloud from a play of their choice; two of the students teamed up to read from Fugard's *The Island*, and the rest proposed to read scenes from McLaughlin's play to her and hear her response. (Interestingly, by this point, the students had little problem with McLaughlin's transposition of Ajax into AJ, a female soldier.)

The result was an exhilarating culmination of the semester's collective effort to think with and through the plays we had read together. As the conversation unfolded, the students and Ellen McLaughlin shared their experiences of Athenian drama's distinctive power to raise vital, critical questions for a whole community – and to speak to audiences and playwrights of our contemporary moment. In our syllabus we had formulated some of these questions: What is justice? What are the appropriate uses of power, and who holds it? What happens when family loyalties and the claims of comradeship clash with established civil laws? How does war affect communities and families? Does it bring them together or divide them?

One of our key surmises proved accurate in both courses; that is, although our prison students' thinking was sophisticated, we surmised that their academic writing skills would be weak.

This was compounded by the fact that although all had GED equivalents and had taken some sort of writing course, many had left formal schooling at age 12 or 13. And the prison library lacked even a basic high-school writing handbook. Given our students' lack of both experience and resources, we had to consider different strategies to improve their writing.

We could write in corrections, but at the same time it was crucial to be respectful of adult students who were doing their best to express themselves in a form not readily available to most of them. We tended to address the grammatical issues one at a time as a brief "sidebar" at the beginning of class. Larger issues of structure could be tackled directly. It took several weeks for everyone to respond to our repeated pleas, "Give your paper a specific title." But eventually the practice caught on, its utility emerged, and often creativity shone out. Paragraphing was a similar challenge. We never deployed the term "topic sentence," but the "one idea at a time" notion gradually took hold.

In general, we corrected everything in their written work but graded solely on their organization and thinking, with emphatic enthusiasm whenever they avoided plot summary or offered a specific quotation from the text that was evidence for an argument. Indeed, we commented on each paper but only assigned grades at the end of the term:

the highest grades for everyone who came to class, discussed, and turned in papers, somewhat lower for students who had not kept up with the reading or handed in all the papers, and lower (though passing) grades for men who had missed a number of classes (some because of disciplinary sequestering) and papers, but were otherwise involved.

Commuting to class was a two-to-three-hour trial each way. On the way up, we complained bitterly. (On the way back, we kept repeating, "It was so worth it!") Our students appreciated that we traveled a considerable distance to spend time with them. In addition to our alliance with Homer and the tragedians, we bridged a gap besides that of millennia. When, in the first class, the men asked, "What shall we call you?" we simply answered with our first names. Titles and degrees had no priority. We all joked a lot.

Will any of these students go on to take more courses or earn degrees?

> *Thank you for turning my foolishness into understanding the meaning of the world in which we live. As I thought of giving up on my education, this course was the reason that a decision for me to continue was made.*

> *Thank you so much for giving me the chance to learn about the Greeks. This class has also helped me, my growth as a student. I'm about to get out so I will see you on campus.*

For some of the students, further education was clearly a great opportunity. For us, however, the whole point became what went on inside the classroom every week. Students, teachers, authors – all struggling with the human condition, together. The surprises we encountered taught us that we needed to examine our surmises – even the ones that proved accurate. What were they based on? What did we take for granted or begin by being oblivious to? These questions remain part of our ongoing reflections, between ourselves and with our students, as we look forward to future courses.

Our most recent students presented each of us, at the last class, with a large sheet of paper. On one side was a drawing – Athena and the Parthenon; Oedipus and the Sphinx – 'commissioned' by our men from other inmates who were artists. On the reverse, our students had written comments to us, a few of which are reproduced above. We close with a selection of some of the others:

I've learned so much about myself and also about Greek because Greek mythology is relevant to society/today.

This course is so meaningful to life. Thank you for your time and efforts in teaching.

To the two wonderful women that enlighten us to understand Greek tragedy which at first I was like what, and then the helpful feedback that you guys give us is very helpful. Keep up the good work and God bless both of you guys.

You have enriched my understanding of Ancient Greek Drama. A direct result of your efforts have enriched my life itself.

You open my world to a new place and help me to find a new way to use my voice in this world and seeing that some battles that were fought in the past are the same today.

We could say the same. Teach in a prison; it will open your world.

5 Inside out: classical myth in a county jail

Alexandra Pappas

CeCe McDonald, a Black trans woman and activist who was imprisoned for defending herself against a racist and transphobic attack, and who at the time of writing was an Activist-in-Residence at the Barnard Center for Research on Women and a 2019 Soros Fellow, speaks to the power of imagination, myth, and education in promoting the agency and freedom of those who are locked up:

> When I was in prison I would sit in my cell and think about how, if I got struck by lightning, maybe I would gain superpowers so I could start kicking down all these walls. This was my form of imaginative abolition, but I also apply it to real life. For me kicking down the walls is educating people, and constantly educating myself.[1]

She thus captures the main themes of this chapter, which details my experiences teaching a 12-week Classical Mythology course of my design in the gender nonconforming pod at the San Francisco County Jail, 2017–18. I review the factors that led to my offering the course, including the essential role of Rhodessa Jones and the women of the Medea Project: Theatre for Incarcerated Women/HIV Circle, with whom I have had the great fortune to work since 2016. I also discuss how the sex- and gender-identities of the students themselves – the majority of whom identify as trans women – shaped the course topics, including our attention to goddesses before gods and to the gender-bending tales of Tiresias, Dionysus, and Hermaphroditus. I include a number of the in-class exercises used to engage the students, and I share their range of responses, from the positive and affirming to the critical and sometimes disgusted. This essay is meant to offer one model for how Classics can inform community outreach and engagement; for how this work can be done outside an established program;

and for how such experiences invite critical, personal reflection on one's own place in the field, in the classroom, and in community.[2]

Background

As part of the January, 2016 Annual Meeting of the Society for Classical Studies in San Francisco, CA, Rhodessa Jones and the Medea Project performed to a packed crowd at Glide Memorial Church. Since the 1980s, Jones and the Medea Project have worked out a method that articulates and performs women's personal experiences of trauma for healing purposes, often grounding the performers' own stories in the tales of women from ancient mythology that stage imprisonment, violence, and abuse.[3] Jones also pays critical attention to the traumas that are the consequences of such subjection: further incarceration, illness, self-harm, silence. Articulating personal stories alongside the ancient fabular ones is particularly effective, as the Medea Project attests. Because it can be too painful to approach and investigate trauma head-on, the difficult work often eludes direct examination; as W. H. Auden articulated it, "Truth, like love and sleep, resents/Approaches that are too intense."[4] Jones's method is to present the stories of mythical others first, and then to invite personal exploration in that shared context. "How have we each been a Medea?" she might ask, once the narrative foundation is laid, or "What's in your Pandora's box?" As the work of the Medea Project has long illustrated, such internal investigation and external narration and performance are essential to challenging habituated behaviors and systemic cycles. This is performance art as social activism.

Sitting in their audience for the first time, watching these women stage their personal experiences of trauma, addiction, disease, and incarceration within a framework of Greco-Roman mythology was transformative. I was moved by prison strikes demanding more programming, and was increasingly inclined to evolve from "doing Classics" in the field's traditional modes to doing something *with* Classics more broadly. A natural response, given my training and interests, was to teach on the inside, and Jones and the Medea Project offered a model for how those strands could come together. I was fortunate to become involved in the Medea Project shortly after the Glide performance – at first bringing myths to their work's contemporary themes, and eventually as a performing member of the company.

Although the Medea Project was not working inside the San Francisco County Jail at that time, one of its longtime core members,

Angela Wilson, was the jail's Rehabilitation Services Coordinator. Formerly incarcerated herself in the late 1990s, when she met Jones and joined the Medea Project, she was now in charge of inmate programming. In late 2016, when she learned of my interest in teaching Classics on the inside, she arranged for me to teach my first class as a one-off in the gender nonconforming pod, which Wilson together with Chief Michele Fisher had been instrumental in establishing a couple of years earlier. This pod houses inmates deemed unsafe in the jail's general population, where the risks of rape, violent assault, and extortion are exceedingly high because of their sex- and/or gender-identities, and where there is no gender-specific programming or contact with the gender nonconforming community.[5] Rather than isolate inmates who identify as gay men, trans women, and/or gender non-binary in the name of safety, as the vast majority of carceral institutions do, the gender nonconforming inmates were integrated and housed in the upper level of the reentry pod, with cis men below and a Deputy mediating in between.[6] "I felt like we weren't offering them anything; they're like the forgotten people, in society *and* in jail," explains Wilson. To her, this integrative change was necessary from the perspectives of safety, inclusion, and program development: medicines could now be carefully administered and monitored; a doctor specializing in gender affirming surgery could visit and give information; trans women could access the same clothing as cis women and could buy makeup from commissary; and, crucially, trans women from the community could give workshops, and offer resources and a place to land on the outside.[7] One transformative solution to the disproportionate policing, arrest, and incarceration of queer and trans people suggested by trans activists and scholars Morgan Bassichis, Alexander Lee and Dean Spade is to "build ongoing, accountable relationships with and advocate for queer and trans people who are locked up to support their daily well-being, healing, leadership, and survival; [and] build community networks of care to support people coming out of prison and jail" (Bassichis, Lee, and Spade 2015, 25). Such work had become more feasible in the formally established gender nonconforming pod.

First impressions

Because the majority of the students I would first teach in the pod identified as trans women, I chose to focus on classical myths of sex and gender transformation. In a tiny room within the pod, nine of us spent our two-hour session with the stories of Tiresias and Hermaphroditus. I narrated the myths as told by Apollodorus and Ovid and showed PowerPoint images from Greek vase-painting and sculpture, and I drew on what I had been learning from Jones about how to use myth to invite the essential work of personal investigation. After presenting the myth of Tiresias, who had famously lived as a man and as a woman and therefore had specialized knowledge according to Zeus and Hera, I asked what special wisdom and insights they had as a result of living trans lives: "How are you a Tiresias?," "How and what can you see that others without your perspective cannot?" Their responses were personal, reflective, and deeply insightful. And their very strong reactions to ancient statues of Hermaphroditus after his physical merging with the nymph Salmacis, ranging from the enchanted to the repulsed, ignited a lively debate about displaying and honoring bodies like this – indeed, like some of theirs – about their value, their vulnerability, their beauty, their danger.

I also wanted us to create something together, to add their voices to the literary and material records we had been studying, so I concluded the class with an experimental group writing exercise. I wrote the first line as a prompt and then passed the paper to a student, who wrote the next line and folded the paper over to conceal the line I had written; the paper circulated person-by-person, folded at each turn so that each writer was only able to see and respond to the single line written immediately above. The initial prompt was an excerpt from Chelsea Manning's coming out statement after her sentencing in August 2013: "I want everyone to know the real me."[8] Once we had each written a line, I read the whole to them. They cheered and applauded, especially delighted by the fitting yet unwitting transition from male to female subject:

> *I want everyone to know the real me:*
> *the real me that nobody knows exists*
> *shakes the earth's heart 'til love comes forth*
> *and bears a son.*
> *The boy grew into maturity, strong and healthy,*
> *left home and fell in with thugs,*
> *hung out with thugs and worked the hoe stroll.*
> *She finally grew up and changed her ways.*
> *Today she looks like a model, and for 6 dollars more she can look*
> *like a cheerleader.*

They all signed the story on the bottom half of the page, a material testament to our time together and the themes of ancient and modern transformation we had so fruitfully explored.

Throughout this first class the discussion was extraordinarily engaged, and I was struck by how effectively the myths made it possible to share and reflect on intimate, personal experiences with real depth even on our first meeting. The students repeatedly remarked how unexpected and affirming it was to find that issues at the heart of their own identities were being explored and sometimes even celebrated thousands of years ago. For them, this was a vastly expanded community, and a validating continuity. For me, this was a partial answer to the urgent question of the value of Classics, to whether it is relevant and if so to and for whom. I left the class energized and committed to sustain this work, valuable both for what it might offer those systemically excluded from the Academy and for how, in turn, it might enrich and expand the field from the outside in. Because of the realities of jail bureaucracy and strained resources, it was almost another year before that became possible.

More lessons on the inside

In fall 2017, the Medea Project received a grant from the California Arts Council to address recidivism, and we began holding weekly performance workshops in the San Francisco County Jail for cis and trans women drawn together from all five pods. I participated from September to May, 2018, during which time we developed inmates' performance pieces informed by the myth of Philomela, whose tongue was cut out so she would not tell of her rape, and by the arc of the hero's journey, which in our group became the "shero's" journey.

I emphasized how, in the ancient mythological tradition, Philomela finds a way to accuse her rapist by nonverbal means, weaving a tapestry to publicize her story in pictures. And in the end, after her perpetrator is avenged, she is turned into a bird, forever free and unfettered. Working with this story was especially charged since the timing coincided with the early allegations against Harvey Weinstein and the reenergized MeToo movement founded by civil rights activist Tarana Burke. We used the myth to investigate the participants' own modes of communicating trauma (or not), structures of systemic silencing and what ultimate freedom for each of them looked like.

So too, the hero's journey exercise, with Odysseus as our ancient model, allowed us to explore what it means in our lives now to leave home, face a number of extraordinary challenges, experience and rebound from a metaphorical death, or in our terms a "rock bottom," and eventually return home a wiser, stronger, and more robust human being. This was quite powerful, since many of the workshop participants saw themselves in the middle of this arc, but found it useful to focus on the possibility of its conclusion in a healthy home, however each woman defined that for herself (for a related, though more in-depth, engagement of the *Odyssey* by incarcerated youth, see Price and Morgan, this volume).

This was an equally instructive moment for those of us conducting the workshops: after several weeks discussing, writing, and rehearsing pieces about freedom and home, Jones reminded us that that even upon release, most of these women, especially the women of color, could never really be free – from social and economic subjection,[9] from disproportionate surveillance and policing by the state, from physical and sexual violence, from systemic physical and material precarity. In this vein, poet and trans/queer activist Nat Raha cautions against the liberal myth of enfranchisement, the exceptionalization of struggles and the appropriation and individualization of self-care. Rather, she calls for a radical revision of individual histories and experiences into a collective, "to understand that our individual struggles, the embedding of sadness, the negative affects we turn inward towards our bodies, are about the absence of a sustainable immediate world within which we could really reside" (Raha 2017, 642–3). This throws into high relief the need to use ancient material to investigate not just the personal decisions and actions that bring harm in order to effect personal transformation but also to highlight those structures that perpetuate these cycles. As Spade articulates it, "the emotional or affective registers of neoliberalism are attuned to notions of 'freedom' or 'choice' that obscure systemic inequalities and turn social movements towards goals of inclusion and incorporation and away from demands for redistribution and structural transformation" (Spade 2015, 22). If there are to be solutions, the problems must be clearly identified, and indeed many of the structural problems that indelibly and unevenly contour the distribution of life chances find their roots in classical antiquity.

Ancient Greek and Roman mythology: power, gender, voice

Being back on the inside weekly with the Medea Project meant continued training for me in these investigative techniques, and it also fortuitously connected me with the new programming staff so that I was able to establish my own weekly two-hour Classical Mythology course, again in the gender nonconforming pod. I taught "Ancient Greek and Roman Mythology: Power, Gender, Voice" from November to February, 2017–18. It was not part of the jail's core educational programming, which left me free to design the class however I wished, but it was approved for Advanced English credit through the Five Keys Charter high school degree-granting program that a number of the longer-term inmates take advantage of.

I shaped the course with my students' identities again in mind, intentionally emphasizing goddesses rather than gods in the early weeks, and including topics explicitly relating to sex and gender identity. As articulated in the syllabus, "This course focuses on myths from ancient Greece and Rome, and includes a review of the major goddesses and gods as well as heroines and heroes. Each class meeting uses the stories as an entry point for students to examine their personal relationships to contemporary power structures; to their public and private voices; and to their gender." The weekly topics were:

1. Hera, queen of the gods
2. Athena, goddess of wisdom and craft
3. Aphrodite, goddess of lust and love
4. Artemis, goddess of virginity and hunting
5. Demeter, goddess of fertility; Persephone, goddess of maidenhood
6. Dionysus, god of transformation and gender-bending
7. Plato's origins of human sexualities and love
8. Tiresias, man-woman-man and blind prophet
9. Danaë, imprisonment, banishment, redemption
10. Antigone, family vs. state
11. Cassandra, curse of truth-telling
12. Helen of Troy, "the face that launched a thousand ships"

With fidelity to the Medea Project methodology, I aimed to connect the myths to our lived experiences with in-class activities and homework assignments. During our class on Aphrodite, for example, we did a freewrite and then presented some of the specific ways that the power of the goddess – i.e., sexual attraction, sometimes destructive – has shaped our lives and the lives of our loved ones. And in our class on Dionysus we wrote and critiqued one another's haikus about our own Dionysian qualities. For homework the students wrote letters from Demeter to Persephone, drawing on their own experiences of separation from family. And based on our study of Danaë and Perseus, they wrote about someone or something they have protected fiercely and what the threats were. And they reflected on their relationship to self and others in response to Aristophanes' claim in Plato's *Symposium* that "Love is the name for the desire and pursuit of wholeness" (192e–193a).

Because of the ways the students engaged every week – making direct and meaningful connections to the ancient material, maintaining deep curiosity, exploring difficult life circumstances that had kept them from thriving – this work took on a meaning I had not otherwise known professionally. It also comes with challenges. Because the class was held in jail, where turnover is often much higher than in prison, I never knew how many students I would have from week to week, what reading, writing, and speaking abilities they would bring or what challenges they were currently facing. Some weeks there were as few as three students, others as many as 15, and maybe I had worked with them before, maybe not. This also meant there could be little continuity of content from week to week, making it difficult to build on homework or previous discussions, and requiring the same introductions every week: to me, to them, to what Classics is, to my purpose and intentions in being there, to what the class might offer them.

There is also the challenge of resources: the students had no access to computers, and we were mostly limited to a few sheets of paper and jail-sanctioned golf pencils. I donated as many personal copies of books as possible, but they did not satisfy the need, and they tended to make their way into someone's personal belongings rather than remain available for general use. I had a weekly PowerPoint prepared, which had to be cleared before each class, but sometimes the necessary cables or monitor would disappear, and we could not use it. We met in a very small room in the pod, and its see-through mirrored walls meant distraction for my students: watching what was going on in the pod and in turn being watched by those not in the class. And students were regularly and without warning pulled out of class for meetings with counselors and lawyers, which was disruptive for everyone. There are also the endless rules and surveillance, the byzantine bureaucracies of the jail, the unwritten hierarchies and egos to learn and navigate. And perhaps most challenging, there is the staggering depth of need and the inability to respond fully.

This kind of work creates opportunities for the students to look deeply inside as well as at the external structures that shape their lives, and its efficacy relies in part on the willingness of the teacher to turn herself "inside out" by sharing personal experiences as well, and to maintain active and honest awareness of her privilege and power. Those of us contributing to this volume, for example, benefit professionally from speaking and writing about this work, but no comparable, formal benefits extend to those whose voices are already suppressed and overridden, whom we risk speaking for as we speak about them. How we respond to this fundamental inequity will depend on the specific contexts of our work – does the carceral institution allow broad internal circulation of student work, e.g., in the form of a zine; does it allow external publication of student voices, whether in writing or a podcast; does our employing institution have a platform for promoting these voices, and if not, can one be created; can we directly connect students with community resources so they have a place to land once released? The particulars will vary, but it is essential for any of us engaged in this kind of pedagogy to maintain such critical reflection and awareness, and to take appropriate action.

This work has revivified Classics for me. I have seen firsthand that it is as beneficial to those newly reached as it is to the field itself and those of us who sustain it. Such direct engagement with our local communities forges meaning outside the ivory tower and invigorates a broader understanding of why Classics matters, and the ways in which it can matter. I conclude with a few excerpted words from the students themselves, who make an utterly compelling case: "Like the story of King Acrisius, sometimes in life we get so consumed by our (good or bad) intentions, we don't think rationally, and we end up making bad decisions that impact our lives in a negative way. We do this out of fear, sometimes for ourselves and sometimes for the ones we love," writes one student. And another reflects:

> I feel so hopeless and powerless at times, because my options are so limited. The whole thing just angers me at times. But I know if I act out in anger I will lose all my options. When I get angry at the limited options I have, the story of Demeter is one of the stories I try to learn from. She was so inspirational to me how she was able to resolve her issues and come up with a compromise without having to revert to violence. In my opinion, she "worked smarter not harder" and she has become my role model and my inspiration.

And, finding resonance in the challenge the suitors posed to Telemachus, another student ponders, "Ignore my issues by not accepting my character defects and therefore allowing them to consume my home and my life? Or set sail and change my future by setting things right in my life ..." Such worthwhile reflection seems precisely what our ancient authors and artists called for, and what Classics continues to be good for.

Notes

1 McDonald 2015, 2. For more on McDonald, see, e.g., *FREE CeCe!*, a 2016 documentary directed by Jacqueline Garas and produced and narrated by Laverne Cox.
2 I am indebted to those without whom this work would not be possible: Rhodessa Jones, Co-founder of Cultural Odyssey and Director of the Medea Project; the women of the Medea Project: Hazel Betsey, Felirene Bongolan, Chibueze Crouch, Theresa Dickinson, Lisa Frias, Shea James,

Deborah King, Muse Lee, Uzo Nwankpa, Felicia Scaggs, Ajahbrielle Sheppard, Cassandra Steptoe, Marlene Stoeckl, and Angela Wilson; the cohorts of students on the inside, whose names are restricted from publication; artist-activist-scholars Diana Cage and Maxe Crandall; and Nancy Rabinowitz, who organized the 2016 SCS performance by the Medea Project as well as the *Classics and the Incarcerated: Methods of Engagement* panel at the 2019 SCS, where I spoke on "Classical Myth on the Inside: Lessons from a County Jail"; and my fellow panel participants there: Sara Ahbel-Rappe, Elizabeth Bobrick, Nancy Felson, Emily Allen-Hornblower, and Jessica Wright.

3 For the methodology created by Jones and the Medea Project's engagement with ancient mythologies, see Fraden 2001; Warner 2004; Rabinowitz 2008 and 2013; Pappas and Jones 2017.

4 Auden, *The Double Man*: quoted in Van der Kolk 2014, 127.

5 Wilson, personal interview, September 26, 2019.

6 I adhere to the definitions laid forth by Lamble 2015, 289, n. 3: "queer" refers to those whose sexual desires, identities, and practices do not conform to heterosexual norms, including lesbian, gay, bisexual, transgender, etc.; "trans" refers to those who express gender differently than what is traditionally associated with the sex assigned at birth; and "gender nonconforming" refers to those whose gender identity or expression does not conform to gender norms, for example "masculine" women, and androgynous, gender-fluid, and gender ambiguous people.

7 Including, for example, representatives from TGIJP, the Transgender Gender-Variant and Intersex Justice Project: http://www.tgijp.org/.

8 https://www.today.com/news/i-am-chelsea-bradley-mannings-full-statement-6C10974052.

9 I follow Spade 2015, 6 in the use of "subjection" rather than "oppression," since it points up how "power relations impact how we know ourselves as subjects through these systems of meaning and control – the ways we understand our own bodies, the things we believe about ourselves and our relationships with other people and institutions, and the ways we imagine change and transformation."

Works cited

Bassichis, Morgan, Alexander Lee, and Dean Spade. 2015. "Building an Abolitionist Trans and Queer Movement with Everything We've Got." In *Captive Genders*, edited by Eric A. Stanley and Nat Smith, 21–46. Edinburgh, Oakland, Baltimore: AK Press.

Fraden, Rena. 2001. *Imagining Medea: Rhodessa Jones and Theater for Incarcerated Women*, with Foreword by Angela Y. Davis. Chapel Hill and London: University of North Carolina Press.

Lamble, Sarah. 2015. "Transforming Carceral Logics: 10 Reasons to Dismantle the Prison Industrial Complex Using a Queer/Trans Analysis." In *Captive Genders*, edited by Eric A. Stanley and Nat Smith, 269–99. Edinburgh, Oakland, Baltimore: AK Press.

62 *Alexandra Pappas*

McDonald, Cece. 2015. "Foreword." In *Captive Genders*, edited by Eric A. Stanley and Nat Smith, 1–3. Edinburgh, Oakland, Baltimore: AK Press.

Pappas, Alexandra, and Rhodessa Jones. 2017. "Not Your Mother's Theater: Rhodessa Jones and the Medea Project." In *Open Space*, "Conversations." San Francisco Museum of Modern Art, June 28, 2017. https://openspace.sfmoma.org/2017/06/not-your-mothers-theater-rhodessa-jones-and-the-medea-project/.

Rabinowitz, Nancy Sorkin. 2008. "The Medea Project for Incarcerated Women: Liberating Medea." *Syllecta Classica* 19: 237–54.

Rabinowitz, Nancy Sorkin. 2013. "Ancient Myth and Feminist Politics: The Medea Project and San Francisco Women's Prisons." In *Roman Literature, Gender and Reception: Domina Illustris*, edited by Donald Lateiner, Barbara K. Gold, and Judith Perkins, 267–83. New York: Routledge.

Raha, Nat. 2017. "Transfeminine Brokenness, Radical Transfeminism." *South Atlantic Quarterly* 116 (3): 632–46.

Spade, Dean. 2015. *Normal Life: Administrative Violence, Critical Trans Politics, and the Limits of Law*, Revised and Expanded Edition. Durham and London: Duke University Press.

Stanley, Eric A., and Nat Smith, eds. 2015. *Captive Genders: Trans Embodiment and the Prison Industrial Complex*, Expanded Second Edition. Edinburgh, Oakland, Baltimore: AK Press.

Van der Kolk, Bessel. 2014. *The Body Keeps the Score: Brain, Mind, and Body in the Healing of Trauma*. New York: Penguin Books.

Warner, Sara L. 2004. "Mythic Theater for Incarcerated Women." *Feminist Studies* 30 (2): 483–509.

6 From family violence to civic order: ancient myths and modern theory in a medium-security prison

Stephen Scully

A young faculty member in the mid 1980s and still very much finding my way in the classroom, I jumped at the opportunity when a professor in the English department asked if I would teach at MCI-Norfolk Prison in Boston University's Prison Program. The invitation came from Elizabeth Barker, whom the inmates called Ma Barker after the famed fugitive who led a band of desperadoes across the Midwest during the Depression. She wore the moniker with pride. A passionate advocate for prisoner education, she believed in its power, especially in the Humanities, to transform individuals and to reduce rates of recidivism.

MCI-Norfolk is a medium-security prison, but it also housed a large number of first and second degree "lifers." Many were serving long sentences, but most would be released one day and returned to society. What better way to prepare them for release than education, especially in the Humanities (see "Liberal Arts," below)? According to a United States Sentencing Commission Report (2016), the recidivism rate for prisoners without a high-school education is a staggering 60%, but for those who had earned a college degree (Bachelors or Associates) in prison that rate fell to under 20%.[1] Although there are no statistics from the 1970s and 1980s to confirm Barker's claim, she used to report that the recidivism rate for BU graduates from Norfolk was under 5%. Barker was fond of saying: "It isn't that no one ever gets arrested again. But it's usually something like a parole violation. The important thing is that none of our guys have hurt people after they have been released."[2] She liked to add: "Prisons that don't help people change their lives aren't tough on crime. They are tough on society."[3]

Barker's belief in prisoner education grew incrementally. As faculty mentor for Boston University's *GE College Bowl* team, she scheduled a practice session with the prisoners at MCI-Norfolk. Impressed by the inmates' intelligence and thirst for learning, she received permission in 1972 from BU's new president, John Silber, to teach college-level courses on a volunteer basis at MCI-N. Within a few years, Barker developed a full-fledged BU program offering a Bachelors of Arts in Liberal Studies for prisoners at Norfolk. In short order, she added a BU MA in Liberal Studies.[4] Today, the program runs on two campuses: MCI-Norfolk for men and MCI-Framingham for women, all expenses – faculty salaries, students' books, administrative overhead – funded by the university. There were no Pell grants or other forms of outside funding.

I quickly signed on to offer a course during the summer (an option no longer available) on mythology, a course I entitled "From Family Violence to Civic Order."

My motives were complex. I had a deep curiosity about – and, I'd say, a healthy fear of – prison. Like others in my generation with a high draft number, it wasn't so many years before that jail loomed as a real possibility for me. It's unlikely that I would have been placed in a medium security prison, but I had to contemplate being locked up. I also wondered about the men inside. How had they crossed the line, committing crimes that would put them away? What if my circumstances had been different?

More importantly, I had recently read Gustave de Beaumont's and Alexis de Tocqueville's *On the Penitentiary System in the United States and its Application in France* (1833) and was aware of what they had considered the proud history that the US, and Massachusetts in particular, had played in prison reform. The MCI of MCI-Norfolk stands for Massachusetts Correctional Institute, the current label in keeping with that nineteenth-century vision that prison was a place both of punishment and of reformation. Since the 1830s, the Commonwealth has abandoned the profoundly misguided idea that solitary confinement provided a proper mixture of punishment and penitential soul-searching, but I was eager to see what the new models of reform and rehabilitation were. I was also aware that the many structural inequities in our society contribute to incarceration, but, even given the systemic flaws in the American penal system, I deeply believed, as did Elizabeth Barker, in the transformative power of education for all, including the incarcerated. BU's low recidivism rate lent credence to the idea that education could elevate, nurture, and provide a pathway to a life without crime. What better way to transform, I thought, than through the hard work of a course: the reading of complex texts, open discussion and the opportunity to express oneself about them in writing?

But, ultimately, I was drawn to teach this course at Norfolk as I was aware that with a prison population serving long sentences, most of my students would have been convicted either of major drug dealing or violent crime, acts often committed against members of one's immediate family not unlike those that we would be reading about in the ancient myths.

My texts included the Babylonian creation myth, the *Enuma elish*, Hesiod's *Theogony*, Genesis, chaps. 1–5, Aeschylus' *Oresteia*, Sophocles' *Oedipus Tyrannus*, Euripides' *Medea* and *Bacchae*, and Homer's *Odyssey*. As a complement to these texts, we would read Freud's *Civilization and Its Discontents*. This last text was not selected as a secondary source but as a twentieth-century version of a creation myth, what Freud himself called a "scientific myth." Now even many years later, only a few other experiences in the classroom have been as intense or enriching for me.

Getting in

It was already past nine and I was late for my first class. Passing through the three "traps" had taken longer than I anticipated. First, guards examined each of my loose-leafed papers and combed through my books, searching for money and other contraband. For each trap, the door behind me had to shut and be locked before the door in front would open. All the while cameras were surveying my movements. Finally through security and for the first time inside the grassy yard, I had to wait for a guard to escort me to my classroom, several brick buildings away. On the perimeter were 19-foot high brick walls, rimmed with barbwire and punctuated with lookout towers with guards bearing rifles. The classroom turned out to be on the second floor, a large room with high ceilings and tall windows, plenty of light, facing the inner yard.

I had been anxious for weeks about first impressions. What would be my first words? How would I introduce myself? What would my students look like? A guard opened the door for me to enter. Inside, the sun flooded the room with light, the air was warm but not too hot, and the room was packed with students, sitting on normal-fare student chairs with a tablet arm for note taking. Other than these students being older, everything looked familiar. Suddenly, it came to me what to say. A few minutes late and walking towards my desk, I turned to the class with a faint smile and said: "It's hard to get in here." To which someone quickly shot back: "It's harder to get out." I knew we were off to a good start.

Lessons learned

1 Tested

Hardly three minutes into my opening comments, a student a little off to the left, on the side opposite from the windows and several rows back, interrupted my spiel, without raising his hand. He held a flyer advertising the course in his hand. Holding it at some distance from his body – the way an actor might when reading a public proclamation – he read the title of the course aloud, pausing after each word: "FROM FAMILY VIOLENCE TO CIVIC ORDER" and then asked in an incredulous tone: "What does that mean?" When I titled the course, I felt I was challenging my students (this material could be hard sledding for some); now the tables were turned. It wasn't difficult to see that this was a make or break moment. He, and really the whole class, was taking my measure. Fair enough.

I lay the syllabus down and started talking to the class, explaining how I related the course title to our readings. I made a point of saying at all times that I was talking about myth, describing how ancient creation stories in particular depicted violence within the nuclear family: fathers hating sons, sons hating fathers, and mothers and fathers at war with each. Sometimes, I said, these stories were explicit about sexual unions, sometimes not, but always the violence was swift and bloody: sons castrating fathers and taking their power, fathers swallowing sons, mothers turning against fathers. I further suggested that these myths implied that such explosive violence was endemic to the family dynamic, part of its DNA, if you will. More than love or nurturing care, it defined the primordial family. This is tough stuff for anyone to hear, but for this population in particular I wanted to stress that these were stories, ways for societies to explain why it was necessary to create new civic orders that might tame primal forces, bringing stability and communal harmony.

I also repeated that I was offering a general outline of recurring themes in Near Eastern and Greek myth, but that each story tells its own story in its own way. Our job in class would be to see how each myth works. We would study the divine family trees, we would talk about each of the gods individually, and we would compare the narrative arc in each myth, studying symbols and metaphors in each, looking for similarities and differences. In short, I invited the students to participate in a semester of close reading.

All of this took a good deal of time. I could tell that my account of hot familial emotions erupting into violence shook the class. If in the beginning the students may have been skeptical about these ancient stories, now they were curious. It was a start. I sensed that they knew something about the explosive interactions I had been discussing. Studying the nuclear family not as a place of love and nourishment but of deadly conflict seemed to have resonated with the group. What initially appeared to be generational strife, initiated by a father fearful of displacement, made a kind of sense. Then to see that this level of conflict give way to a deeper gender conflict between the parents over the children made even more sense. As with all classes, aware that some in the class may have experienced these violent forces first hand, I was always careful to stress that I was talking about stories, ancient myths. I felt that this was the best way to get us to look and to read closely.

I seemed to have passed the first test, but it wouldn't be the last. I had never laid out the themes of a course so openly at the beginning of a class before. I worried that I had shot my wad. I feared that the rest of the semester would be anticlimactic, but, of course, that was wrong. We came back to these patterns again and again over the semester, but each time the dynamic was different and the conversation fresh.

As a new teacher, I had learned a lesson. Get to the heart of the matter quickly.

2 Freud

Turning from Babylonian and Greek creation myths to Freud was another memorable moment. When I walked into the classroom that morning, a student in the back of the room was standing on his chair, body fully erect, with his right hand raised above his head and in his fist Freud's text was crumbled into a ball. As I walked to my desk, he yelled out in full voice at me: "How dare Freud say that man is naturally violent." I turned to him as calmly as I could and replied: "It's a theory. Let's look at it." And so we did for 90 minutes before we took our break, at which point another student came up to me and said: "Reading Greek myth was hard enough, but Freud cuts too close to the bone."

I learned so much about the power of story that day. While much of "the family romance" in *Civilization and Its Discontents* replicates stories from myth, the two genres are miles apart. Even though I am inclined to read Freud's text as a fictive construct, he regards it as a story about the origins and development of civilization based upon discoveries first made by psychoanalytic research of the self. As such, his story claims the objective authority of observed phenomena and, unlike myth, mixes narrative with declarative statements. It is one thing to read stories, especially from people long ago and far away who believed in strange gods; these stories can speak to us but they clearly are not our stories. It is another thing for Freud to make pronouncements about the human condition and to proclaim psychological truths as universal. It is Freud's truth-claim that hit the students at Norfolk so hard. They lived in a world where guards and other members of their community repeatedly called them "animals" and some of them feared, as one told me privately, that a fierce animal might indeed lie within. For them, more than for most, Freud's claim *homo homini lupus,* that man is a wolf to man, was too much to bear. This is a difficult statement for anyone to read, and always leads to a great deal of discussion in any class, but for this population the psychoanalytic "truth-claim" was especially harsh. As the student said at the break, it cut too close to the bone. After the break, we spent an hour discussing the idea and what Freud meant by it.

The comparative reaction to the myths and Freud made me understand why fifth-century Athenians made it a policy to avoid current history and painful Athenian stories in their productions of tragedy in the City Dionysia. Recent history for them, like Freud's claims, was too painful to witness; tragedy was more effective if it told stories of heroes from a remote past, and even better if these stories took place outside of Athens, as most tragedies did (Troy, Thebes, and Mycenae being favored locales).

3 Literature as propaganda: Odysseus

In the early years, the BU program picked a prisoner to serve as a "clerk," a teacher's assistant who distributed the books to the class and helped keep the students on track between classes. In later years, the program abandoned this position as the clerks sometimes took on airs and felt superior to the other students. In my time, the clerk was very large – easily 6'4" and 250 lbs. – and very soft-spoken. He was a Black Panther, incarcerated for killing an FBI infiltrator in San Francisco. It's very possible that the person he killed had sat next to me in study hall when I was in the eighth-grade. My classmate grew up to be an FBI investigator who had infiltrated the Panthers with hostile intent and was killed in San Francisco. This eerie coincidence was often on my mind. Though the clerk liked to call me "dear" and was a genuinely helpful and thoughtful assistant, I sensed a fury behind the gentleness. He also hated Odysseus and the *Odyssey* with a passion, finding it pure propaganda for white supremacy and western imperialism. The *only* figure in the poem he admired was a Semitic slave-girl from Sidon who sold Eumaeus to the pirates and ran off with them (*Odyssey* 15.417–81). In these 60 lines he saw the potential for a non-western heroine. He was furious with Homer for killing her off so quickly, jettisoning her from the story with a brush of the hand. Without a doubt, this was the most intense and sustained discussion of a passage that I have ever experienced in an "undergraduate" classroom.

4 Spontaneity

More than any other course that I have taught, student responses in this classroom were transparent. It was never difficult for me to know if I was teaching well or not. If we were together as a group, you could have heard a pin drop in the back of the room, so rapt was their attention; if I had lost their interest, it was close to pandemonium. My students at BU were always more measured. I came to love this openness at Norfolk as the students let me know at all times if I was on point. As much as I loved my students' spontaneity and quick responsiveness, it also made me wonder if under other circumstances this openness could have dire consequences. To the question I had asked myself before classes began – would these students somehow look different – the answer was definitely, no. They wore prison blue jeans, but otherwise they looked like anyone else. But I was anxious that maybe in other settings such quick responses might lead to trouble.

Aftermath

1 Odyssey

A year or two after I left, a student in the class created a national prison journal to "reflect on the essence of the prison experience – the journey home," as he described it. Inspired by the story of Odysseus, he called it simply *Odyssey*. It met with some resistance from prison officials (cf. Janusz 1993). This student was remarkably sharp and articulate, but he never found it easy to conform to higher ups or to follow the rules. A few years later when he was released from Norfolk, we saw each other several times, but, when he realized that I couldn't get him a position in the university, he wandered off. He never did make it home. In relatively short order, he was back behind bars where, not many years later, he died. Education did not save him from being one of the 5% repeat offenders.

2 Liberal arts

I only taught this course once, but I went back to MCI-N on multiple occasions for several years. Prisoners frequently asked Ma Barker about me and I saw them – at least those who hadn't been transferred or weren't in solitary – at poetry readings there.

I also attended BU graduation ceremonies at MCI-N where I came to understand the term Liberal Arts in a new way. We think of the Liberal Arts as implying leisure, used to describe non-practical training in the university. But from my experience at Norfolk, I began to think of liberal as a verbal adjective, conveying that an education in the Humanities, and stories in particular, has a liberating effect upon the person.

Our readings gave the students a way to see that they were not alone in the world, that other human beings from across the globe and across time had similar experiences or feelings as they. Many prisoner testimonials have spoken to the liberating effect of reading. One that particularly stands out for me comes from Walter Rideau. He experienced that liberation as a gradual emergence from the co-coon of self-centeredness and an awakening of a new perspective of self. He writes:[5]

> Angola introduced me to the idea of reading just to kill time. The first book I read was *Fairoaks*, a historical novel by Frank Yerby [about] "how white folks been messing over our people," [as one of the inmates had described the book. Such topics] had never received more than a passing mention in the history classes I attended. But this book brought it to life and ignited something in me. I wanted to know more – about slavery, about history, and, ultimately, about everything. From then on, I lived inside my head, in a world of books. It helped me survive

the maddening monotony and boredom of the cell. Except for the unrelenting need for sexual relief and the periodic need to stretch my legs and exert myself physically, I buried myself in books. Reading obscured the dismal future I faced. Initially, I read whatever was available on the black market – smuggled books – or those owned by other death row inmates. After a prison library was created, I could be more selective, choosing what I wanted from the book cart brought in by a trusty. The more I learned, the more I sought; the more I reflected, the more I grew and matured. There were no lightning bolts, instant revelations, or overnight conversions; it was a long growth process in which I began to shed the ignorance, anger, and insecurities that had governed my previous life. I learned more from my reading on death row than I had during all my years of formal schooling, which had left me literate but uneducated. Eventually, I came to see that there was so much more to life and to the world, so many options available that, as bad as things might have been, I was never as trapped in life as I had believed. I realized that my real problem had been ignorance and, as a result, I had thrown away my life.

Reading ultimately allowed me to feel empathy, to emerge from my cocoon of self-centeredness and appreciate the humanness of others [...] It enabled me finally to appreciate the enormity of what I had done.

I saw the humanities as freeing one from the prison-house of the self. The stories we were reading gave these students a way to move outside of themselves, to see their own experiences from a distance, and to scrutinize them from afar. Such an experience could also lead to empathy, an awareness that others may have walked down similar paths. This kind of liberation could happen anywhere, even in prison. It was a form of freedom that could not easily be taken away.

Notes

1 US Sentencing Commission report 2016, 24. For the different levels of prison education and for methodological difficulties in evaluating the out-comes, see Gaes 2008, Davis et al. 2013, and Scott 2018. Castro 2018, 13 duly cautions: "Expanded access to quality education during incarceration is necessary but it should not be seen as 'purely instrumental'."

2 Quoted in Barker's Obituary, *Boston Globe*, February 23, 2001. Of course, this is a select population and many factors, in addition to education, affect recidivism. Reliable sources tell me that Barker's estimate of 5% recidivism was accurate, if not a little high. Cf. Brown 2019.

3 Cf. http://www.bu.edu/bridge/archive/2001/03–09/obituary.html (*BU Bridge*, March 9, 2001). Boston University (cf. Boston University. Metropolitan College) describes the Prison Education Program as follows: "[W]e believe in the power of education to elevate, nurture, and transform ... Rigorous study gives prisoners the intellectual leverage and self-confidence they need to re-form their view of themselves and leave prison better equipped to contribute positively to their families and communities."

4 Since 1972 from the combined programs, 372 inmates have earned a BU BA, 50 of these also getting a MA. 25 inmates have received MAs only. The MA program was phased out, starting in 1989.

5 Rideau 2010, 45-6. Rideau was on death row from 1961 to 1972 at Angola Prison in Louisiana. From 1975 to 1995, he was editor of *The Angolite*. He was released from prison in 2005.

Works cited

Boston University. Metropolitan College. n.d. "Prison Education Program." Accessed July 17, 2019. http://sites.bu.edu/pep/.

Brown, Joel. 2019. "Behind Bars. And Graduating from BU. Prison Education Program. Steven Correia's story shows why it matters." *BU Today*, May 15, 2019. http://www.bu.edu/articles/2019/prison-education-program-graduation/.

Castro, Erin. 2018. "Racism, the Language of Reduced Recidivism, and Higher Education in Prison: Toward an Anti-Racist Praxis," *Critical Education* 9, no. 17: 1–19.

Davis, Lois M., Robert Bozick, Jennifer L. Steele, Jessica Saunders, and Jeremy N. V. Miles. 2013. *Evaluating the effectiveness of correctional education: A meta-analysis of programs that provide education to incarcerated adults*. Santa Monica, CA. RAND Corporation.

Gaes, Gerald. 2008. *The impact of prison education on post-release outcomes* (Reentry Roundtable on Education, John Day College of Criminal Justice in New York City, 2008. http://www.antoniocasella.eu/nume/Gaes_2008.pdf.

Janusz, Luke. 1993. "*Odyssey*: A Prison Magazine's Difficult Journey," *The National Prison Project, Journal* 8: 1–2 and 21. https://www.prisonlegalnews.org/media/publications/journal%208-1.pdf.

Obituary of Elizabeth Barker, *BU Bridge,* March 9, 2001. http://www.bu.edu/bridge/archive/2001/03–09/obituary.html

Obituary of Elizabeth Jackson "Ma" Barker, *Boston Globe,* February 23, 2001. https://bostonglobe.newspapers.com/image/442229286/?terms=Elizabeth%2BBarker

Rideau, Wilbert. 2010. *In the Place of Justice: A Story of Punishment and Deliverance*. New York: Vintage Books.

Scott, Robert. 2018. "The Concept of Reducing Recidivism via College-in-Prison: Thoughts on Data Collection, Methodology and the Question of Purpose," *Critical Education* 9, no. 18: 1–15.

United States Sentencing Commission Report 2016. Recidivism Among Federal Offenders: A Comprehensive Overview. https://www.ussc.gov/sites/default/files/pdf/research-and-publications/research-publications/2016/recidivism_overview.pdf.

Part II
Beyond the classroom

7 Teaching Ovid to incarcerated students: an experiential analysis

Nicole Dib and Olga Faccani

Introduction

A poem about basketball, a short story about the Yukon, and an essay about a weasel are among the topics and genres featured in the "Foundations in the Humanities" prison correspondence course facilitated by the University of California, Santa Barbara's Interdisciplinary Humanities Center (hereafter, IHC). The first iteration of the course was offered to students at the California Men's Colony and Kern Valley State Prison; it has since expanded to Salinas Valley State Prison, Soledad Correctional Training Facility, and other locations. These correspondence courses are taught by 6–10 graduate students at UCSB, who apply to be IHC Graduate Teaching Fellows and take a course on pedagogy, prison teaching, and the politics surrounding prisons alongside their correspondence work with students in California prisons. From September 2017 to June 2018, we worked as teaching fellows for "Foundations in the Humanities." As part of the course, students in prison read and responded to questions about six different works, one of which was Ovid's myth titled "Baucis and Philemon."

Ovid's "Baucis and Philemon" travels far over the course of "Foundations in the Humanities"; like Jupiter and his son Mercury, it seeks to be welcomed as it is sent to our students in California prisons and correctional facilities. Our students' engagement with this classical text is clear from their keen responses to it, but teaching the correspondence course made us reflect on our pedagogy and our practice. After a brief introduction on the way the correspondence course worked, we will first explore our students' reactions to Ovid's tale and then our own teaching experience, with special attention to the context of a correspondence course that did not include in-person interactions with students.

The "Foundations in the Humanities" course begins with a visit from IHC Director Susan Derwin, who goes to each prison to teach a class and to encourage interested students to enroll. The students who attend the onsite class send a letter of interest and, once they are accepted into the program, begin to take part. Students' acceptance into the program is determined by a preliminary interview conducted by Professor Derwin, and is contingent upon the number of graduate student instructors who choose to participate in the program: each instructor provides responses to between 5 and 10 incarcerated students. Often, the number of incarcerated students who apply for the program exceeds the number of instructors available; since, however, some students leave the course within the first two to four weeks, others are admitted even after the program has already begun. Once the course begins, students receive their assignments by mail: each reading is sent with a brief summary of the work, basic information about the author and time of composition, and a series of questions. The students mail their answers, which are each to be a minimum of 150 words, back to the IHC, where the Graduate Teaching Fellows read them and write extensive feedback, which is then returned by mail. While "Foundations in the Humanities" does not offer college credits, participation in the course appears on students' records, and can be shown to parole boards.

Given the lack of face-to-face interaction, the questions that accompany each reading play a pivotal role: it is through them that the intellectual trajectory of the course is set. For Ovid's "Baucis and Philemon," we developed questions intended to prompt our students' reflection on concepts central to the text – for instance, hospitality, fair treatment, and the value of sacrifice.

1.   Baucis and Philemon entertained the guests in their home. What did the description of their hospitality reveal about the old man and his wife? When they realized that their guests were Olympian gods, why did they have "no choice" but to kill their beloved goose?
2.   You will notice that the gods have the power to change humans into objects from the natural world, and that, at different moments in the story, things, people, and gods assume new shapes or forms. Describe three moments of transformation and discuss why you think they are significant.
3.   "They were very poor but they had accepted their plight and so they had made light of it." Why do you think the couple was able

to be happy? What do the two wishes they express reflect about their relationship?
4. Three ideas or themes that are central to the story are: the treatment of guests or strangers, the value of sacrifice, and the meaning of gratitude. Say something about how the story represents each of these themes.
5. (Optional). Discuss how the three themes mentioned in question #4 relate to your own life.

We recognize that these questions shaped our students' reading of the text, and necessarily shaped their written responses as well. The guided nature of the correspondence course meant that we were giving our students our version of the story, the framework, and the points of analysis. In an in-person setting, many of the questions we provided as accompaniment to the text would have emerged during our discussion with the students; in the correspondence setting of our course, however, we tried to incorporate our students' perspectives on the text in our feedback to their responses. We felt that these questions adequately guided our students' reflections as they approached the text, leaving at the same time enough room to focus on the aspects of the myth that most resonated to them. We found that some of these questions that asked students to reflect on theme, narrative, and ethics, also fostered metacognitive responses; for example, our question about the couple's happiness despite their poverty prompted our students to offer their thoughts about the very notion of happiness within the context of prison, and the interplay between happiness and sacrifice.

Some prompts, such as question number two about moments of transformation in the myth, necessitated closer readings of the story but still allowed for personal interpretations. In fact, in response to this question, some students wrote about moments of hospitality they encountered inside and outside of prison, and they brought their own experiences to bear on their reading of the text. We also found that, among the 16 students we interacted with during this section of "Foundations in the Humanities," 10 responded to the optional question about the connection between themes present in "Baucis and Philemon" and their own lives. Though small, our sample demonstrates an eagerness and willingness on the part of our students to contribute more than what was required of them in terms of writing and analysis. In their responses to the optional question, our students wrote about their interactions with other incarcerated individuals, and discussed the role of sacrifice, gratitude, and hospitality in their own lives.

Our students' reactions and responses to "Baucis and Philemon"

Even though prison education has often been described as a practice that provides a space for humanization and liberation, several critiques of this narrative have been raised in recent years.[1] In teaching Ovid's myth, we found that students' responses also spoke to the inadequacy of this assumption, and at the same time seemed to give evidence for the relevance of the themes embedded in the text.

"Baucis and Philemon" does not present those themes of aggression and sexual violence that are otherwise pervasive in the *Metamorphoses* and that have made the poem notoriously controversial as a text to be discussed in the classroom.[2] The myth's romantic dénouement – in which the old couple, transformed into entwined trees, find a peaceful end to their days as tenders of the gods' temple – is a far cry from much more famous and violating tree transformations in the poem. In Book 1 of the *Metamorphoses*, for example, Daphne fails to escape Apollo's abuse even in her non-human form, the wood still shrinking from the god's kisses. As our students' responses highlighted, however, the ending of "Baucis and Philemon" – with its celebration of hospitality and altruism – is only apparently positive and reassuring, and offers a context for important reflections on the themes of punishment and gratitude within the praxis of prison education.

Many of our students noted that Ovid's myth ends with a stark juxtaposition: next to Baucis and Philemon in their arboreal form is a dark lake, at the bottom of which lies the town with its inhabitants, punished by the gods. As readers, our students' identification with the characters of Baucis and Philemon in the story was often attenuated by the fact that existence in prison bears more similarities to Ovid's dark lake than his golden temple. One of our students observed that prison represents their dark lake of sufferings, and that, even if they strive to be altruistic in their daily life, they still are at the bottom of the lake. As another student pointed out, it is difficult for acts of generosity to be reciprocated in a prison environment. Much like the townspeople punished by the gods' irrevocable judgment, many of our students knew they would not get a second chance at proving their ability to be kind and altruistic outside prison, but they would spend the rest of their lives incarcerated. While some of our students alluded to the dark lake in Ovid with no possibility of redemption as reminiscent of the condition of life without parole, others reflected on the old couple's agency in their choice to offer the gods their hospitality. On the one hand, Baucis and Philemon were rewarded for their display of altruism; on the other, they had "no choice" but to sacrifice their beloved goose the moment that they recognized the gods disguised as beggars. Many of our students pointed out that they became more grateful of other people's acts of generosity while incarcerated, but their agency and free will in exerting altruistic practices were limited by the constraints of the prison system. From their readings of the myth's juxtapositions, our students demonstrated a range of identifications that helped them question the very notions of hospitality, agency, and punishment in the text.

The correspondence format also influenced our students' approach to the text. Even though, as we mentioned, our questions shaped to an extent their interpretations, our students were able to develop their thoughts without being interrupted by suggestions or comments from teachers or classmates, as commonly occurs in a classroom environment. For this reason, perhaps, students often reflected on the themes embedded in the text in very personal ways, drawing from their past as free individuals and their present reality of incarceration. Such self-reflection was facilitated by the practice of writing rather than sharing their ideas in front of a group, which can be overwhelming. Correspondence, moreover, allowed students to spend the time they needed, or the time they could afford, reflecting on what the text meant for them, and forming their own judgments without the pressure of in-classroom scrutiny.

A severe limitation inherent in the correspondence format was the impossibility of creating a real sense of community among the students – something which we consider one of the main benefits of education whether in carceral or non-carceral spaces.[3] Within the specific context of prison education, building communities also bears a validating purpose for students: for example, one of our students, in their reflection on the theme of generosity in Ovid, shared that they felt validated and encouraged to become more altruistic when they heard the positive reinforcement and approval from other incarcerated individuals. This kind of validation experienced by the student occurred, necessarily, outside the context of our correspondence class, where personal reflections could not be shared with other members of the course.

Moreover, the solipsistic exercise inherent in the correspondence format replicates, to an extent, the structures of separation and isolation that are ingrained in the prison system. At the same time, the freedom resulting from the absence of those boundaries that, in an in-person setting, are dictated by the teachers' and classmates' interventions or suggestions, introduces an element of subversive agency within the very context of the prison system. Like all education, then, there are mixed advantages and disadvantages.

Teaching dynamics and learning: our experiential analysis

Teaching incarcerated students proved to be a different experience from our usual pedagogical encounters. Teaching via mail meant adopting a new mindset regarding the student–teacher relationship, and adapting as well to the prison setting. The power imbalance that already underlies the teacher–student hierarchy is emphasized in the prison setting by the instructors' position as free outsiders and the students' position as incarcerated insiders. Correspondence courses add, then, an additional layer of separation where there already is one between student and teacher in the prison pedagogy scenario. There was a level of anonymity put into place both by the lack of a classroom and by the pseudonyms, required in our course, we (as instructors) used in our correspondence; our students, however, shared their real names with us. As other essays in this collection discuss (for instance, the one by Jessica Wright), there is an imbalanced dynamic that is an inseparable part of any prison education course.

At the same time, we found that the correspondence nature of our course did allow for humanistic thinking and feedback-based interaction with students who might not be able to attend traditional classrooms. Indeed, although we were cognizant of the power dynamic, we also recognized that our course was uniquely able to continue to be offered throughout difficult or unusual circumstances. Students did not have to abide by a strict schedule of in-person classes, which often proves difficult to adhere to within the unpredictable and constrictive environment of prison. On several occasions, our students mailed their responses late due to solitary confinement, or unforeseen transfers to different facilities, but such inconveniences did not preclude them from participation in the course the same way they would have with an in-person prison education format. Prison lockdowns also play a role here – our students could continue to read, write, and receive our correspondence throughout these often untimely situations.

In a more drastic example of our course's efficacy during unforeseeable disruptions, during the COVID-19 pandemic Nicole – who continued to teach the course and its sequels to approximately 30 students in 2020 – was able to maintain her correspondence throughout the crisis. In a different context, Olga also adjusted to the pandemic and foregrounded students' personal experiences and reflections as she developed an online course focused on ancient Greek play *Trojan Women* for female incarcerated students at the Ventura Youth Correctional Facility. The course, which was originally meant to be offered in person, could still be offered inside the prison as a hybrid correspondence course: the incarcerated students were able to follow some classes online via Zoom, and would submit their reflections on the themes in the play as scanned writings, that the instructors would receive via email. Thus, in this exceptional circumstance, the lack of in-person contact with the students – which, as we discuss below, led to most of the challenges we faced during the academic year 2017–18 – was the very feature that allowed us to keep teaching.

We found the most jarring difference between teaching in person and teaching via correspondence to be our inability to process, together with our students, the text at hand. Rather than starting a discussion with an open-ended or more reflective question about their experience with the text, our questions, as listed above, prompted analysis right away. The first question, for example, required students to analyze Ovid's description of Baucis and Philemon's hospitality, then asked them to consider why their hospitality caused them to have "no choice" but to slaughter their precious goose. While this question had an element of objective analysis, since it prompted students to demonstrate their understanding of the main story elements, it also allowed for interpretative freedom and criticism: some students even disagreed with the phrasing of the question, because they felt that Baucis and Philemon *did* have a choice, and that this very choice was part of their own notion of generosity and hospitality.

We realized that the wording of these questions was especially important in a context that left no room for in-person discussion, and that giving our students the possibility to grapple with our guiding questions (rather than asking for purely objective information) was a way to render this correspondence course reflective as well as rigorous. It is notable that the lesson we (as early career educators) took from this challenge translates to our traditional classroom setting as well. Nicole, who branched out into teaching writing courses at UCSB shortly after starting her work with the IHC's correspondence course, used this formula of "analysis-meets-reflection" questions to help her first-year composition students learn how to read scholarly writing in a more engaged way. Rather than quizzing her students on what they learned from readings on genre, rhetorical analysis, and discourse communities, she asked them about their own positions toward the text at hand, and encouraged them to point out where they struggled with, disagreed with, or related to the arguments that rhetoricians made.

During our facilitation of the course, we found that we were able to incorporate our prior experience as Teaching Assistants, Instructors of Record, and other similar positions while also adjusting, somewhat drastically, the mindset that comes with that experience. We were forced to confront our assumptions about teaching with questions such as: "what does evaluation look like when there are no grades?" or "what does learning look like when there are no prerequisites on which we can build, and no 'later class' that we are preparing our students for?" When Nicole – with her background in English – teaches UCSB's Introduction to Literary Studies course, for example, she expects the students to know how to write for an academic audience, even though she does not expect that they will have knowledge of specifics of literary analysis (which they will gain in the course). Or, when Olga – with her background in Classics – teaches Greek and Roman mythology in traditional classroom settings, she rarely has to reflect, for example, on how the theme of hospitality that animates much of Ovid's story is interpreted differently within a context that drastically limits personal freedom.

The framework of our correspondence course also affected the way we provided our written feedback. Our goal was to deeply engage with our students' thoughts about the text and to provide commentary (and encouragement) on their analyses, while being careful not to insert our own interpretations of the text in our responses. We did not want to be negative or patronizing nor to induce our students to disclose their own experiences as in a therapeutic session. We also chose to minimize correction of errors, because we wanted, as Eleanor Novek (2017, 41) advises, "to build confidence in students alienated by their previous experiences of schooling," so as to enable them "to enjoy self-expression without evaluation." However, if our students' answers wandered too far from the prompts, we would include in our feedback a reminder that they should direct their readings and analyses as much as possible toward the text at hand. As Lockard and Rankins-Robertson (2018, xvi) remark, "teaching incarcerated students (like teaching other students) means much more than simply allowing them to speak without restraint. It is not a matter of stepping outside discipline into free expression. The project instead is to grasp new rules and master new forms." As we mentioned earlier, our prior pedagogical experiences in English and Classics gave us "rules" and "forms" in mind ahead of time; what we had to have in mind during the facilitation of this course, however, was different.

One recurring point in our feedback was our appreciation for our students' focus on the altruism at the heart of Ovid's myth. Our questions did guide them toward that theme, but students often picked up on the less overt mental connection between Baucis and Philemon themselves, demonstrated – they found – by the fact that they agreed on their course of action right away. We also wanted to encourage comparative analyses, by responding to them in our feedback, though we could not expect or specifically prepare for them; for example, a student wrote about how Ovid's myth reminded them of a poem by Chickasaw writer Linda Hogan, and they compared the themes of transformation in the classical myth to Native American poetry. We did expect students to link any related texts or stories to their answers, however, and we simply included a brief reminder to focus as much as possible on our guiding questions if a student wrote a response that was too off-topic. Once again, the lack of room for conversation prompted us to come up with brief ways to try to dialogue with our students.

In our instruction of Ovid's "Baucis and Philemon" we sought to create a space in which our students would feel comfortable engaging with a myth from classical literature in a way that would foreground their experiences and reflections. Teaching Ovid's tale was a way to send a piece of the past – in the form of a story that encourages interpretative freedom – into a system whose existence is antithetical to the ideals of liberation, education, and responsibility to one another. The value of hospitality at the heart of Ovid's myth is one that our students instantly recognized and theorized with their analyses and their personal reflections, and is one that we hope can continue to guide our pedagogy in different spheres of education.

Notes

1 Lockard 2018 examines some of the assumptions underlying prison education programs in the US. For a critique of the notion of prison education as liberating in the present volume, see Jessica Wright's contribution.
2 See, e.g., Kahn 2004; Gloyn 2013; Richlin 2014; Thakur 2014; James 2014; Waldman 2018. For a recent reading of the *Metamorphoses* that challenges misogynistic paradigms from antiquity and promotes empowerment, see Morales 2020, 65–82.
3 Novek 2017 discusses the benefits of creating a community of knowledge among incarcerated students. Her approach builds on Parker Palmer's notion of "community of truth," in which learners are in relationship both to a subject and one another. Muth 2008 further notes that the development of meaningful human connection among incarcerated individuals generates a "third space" in the prison classroom, where "learners are no longer powerless" (270).

Works cited

Gloyn, Elizabeth. 2013. "Reading Rape in Ovid's Metamorphoses: A Test-Case Lesson." *Classical World* 106, no. 4: 676–681.

James, L. Sharon. 2014. "Talking Rape in the Classics Classroom: Further Thoughts." In *From Abortion to Pederasty: Addressing Difficult Topics in the Classics Classroom*, edited by Nancy Sorkin Rabinowitz and Fiona McHardy, 171–186. Columbus: Ohio State University Press.

Kahn, Madeleine. 2004. "'Why Are We Reading a Handbook on Rape?' Young Women Transform a Classic." In *Pedagogy* 4, no. 3: 438–459.

Lockard, Joe, and Sherry Rankins-Robertson, eds. 2018. *Prison Pedagogies: Learning and Teaching with Imprisoned Writers*. Syracuse: Syracuse University Press.

Lockard, Joe. 2018. "Prison Writing Education and US Working-Class Consciousness." In *Prison Pedagogies: Learning and Teaching with Imprisoned Writers*, edited by Joe Lockard and Sherry Rankins-Robertson, 11–31. Syracuse: Syracuse University Press.

Morales, Helen. 2020. *Antigone Rising: The Subversive Power of the Ancient Myths*. New York: Bold Type Books.

Muth, Bill. 2008. "Radical conversations: Part one. Social constructivist methods in the ABE classroom." *The Journal of Correctional Education* 59, no. 2 (September): 261–281.

Novek, M. Eleanor. 2017. "Jail pedagogies: Teaching and Trust in a Maximum-Security Men's Prison." *Dialogues in Social Justice* 2, no. 2: 31–51.

Palmer, Parker. 1998. *The Courage to Teach. Exploring the Inner Landscape of a Teacher's Life*. San Francisco: Jossey-Bass Publishers.

Richlin, Amy. 2014. "Reading Ovid's Rapes." In *Arguments with Silence: Writing the History of Roman Women*, 130–165. Oxford, UK: Oxford University Press.

Thakur, Sanjaya. 2014. "Challenges in Teaching Sexual Violence and Rape: A Male Perspective." In *From Abortion to Pederasty: Addressing Difficult Topics in the Classics Classroom*, edited by Nancy Sorkin Rabinowitz and Fiona McHardy, 152–170. Columbus: Ohio State University Press.

Waldman, Katy. 2018. "Reading Ovid in the Age of #MeToo." *The New Yorker*. February 12, 2018. https://www.newyorker.com/books/page-turner/reading-ovid-in-the-age-of-metoo

8 A poetics of performance liberation: a conversation about *The Odyssey Project*

Michael Morgan and Zachary Price

The Odyssey Project was created in the summer of 2011 by Professor Michael Morgan as a course that partners University of California, Santa Barbara students with incarcerated youth to develop a prison theater intervention program using Homer's epic poem *The Odyssey*. Offered as a class called "The People's Voice" through the Department of Theater and Dance, *The Odyssey Project* began collaborating with the Santa Barbara Department of Youth Probation's Los Prietos Boys Camp (LPBC). The population of LPBC is made up of adolescents aged 13–18. They are considered "wards of the court" who are in a liminal position between going to juvenile hall and going home. Over the six-week class/rehearsal process, the ensemble learns acting, writing and spoken word exercises, mask making, choreography, mime, and martial arts. The six-week engagement culminates in a public performance, including a post-show discussion with ensemble and community members.

As a graduate student at UCSB, I (Zachary) first became involved with *The Odyssey Project* in its inaugural year when Michael engaged me in conversation about creating a social justice program. He shared his desire to establish a platform that would provide a marginalized and non-university community access to university resources. As Black men who developed a Du Boisian "double-consciousness" (Du Bois 1989, 3) to negotiate the constant contradictions of the historically white university environment, Michael and I shared similar experiences. We each had also been introduced to theater as adolescents through outreach programs and thus understood the necessity of creating such platforms for others.

Yet, in June 2020 the streets of the US are ablaze in rebellion over the terrorism of white supremacy in the form of extrajudicial violence and state-sanctioned anti-Black policing. America has the world's largest prison population, one that disproportionately is made up of Black and Latinx people. To be Black is to live in a constant state of terror that you might be incarcerated, maimed, or killed for simply existing. This is what Frank Wilderson (2010) means when he suggests that the ontological experience of Black people within modernity is gratuitous violence. The history of American policing is rooted in protecting the most prized private property that it ever possessed which was Black flesh, and it was the free labor of chattel slavery that gave rise to the economic order of American civil society. Today, civil society demands peaceful demonstration after Black people are murdered, and it simultaneously demands the protection of private property. Hence maintaining order is about perpetuating a structural racial antagonism that slavery produced through what Michelle Alexander (2012) refers to as the "New Jim Crow."

The response to such history means working through difficult and perhaps nearly impossible questions. Is it possible to rehearse for revolution and plan for a different world – a different political, social, economic system? Is it possible to "sneak into the university and steal" (Harney and Moten 2013, 26) what has been stolen in preparation for an equitable future? Is it possible to be in but never of the university and its consolidated power?

This essay is structured as a conversation between Michael and myself. It is intended to be an extension and rejoinder to post-show discussions and a critique of the evolution of *The Odyssey Project* as well as the carceral system. Hopefully it will aid those educators, activists, policymakers, and cultural workers who take seriously the possibilities of using art for what Paulo Freire (2000) referred to as "education as the practice of freedom."

A conversation

Zachary: Why did you decide to go with the *Odyssey* and not a different myth?

Michael: There's a kind of reflection about identity when you are on the margins – considerations about how to get back home and provocations about what home is. Incarcerated youth must look at where they are, where they came from and where they are going. I believe Odysseus is similarly in a situation of exile. This project deals with disenfranchised people. It deals with anyone who has been "othered." It's a mainstream story as a canonical work, but it has entrances for people at the margins and the outskirts. I think people who are not primary voices in society can own it as a narrative. They can breathe fresh life into it. I like the social talkback that this myth provides for people who have been in trouble, displaced, and are in search of a center – a center both inner and outer that they can identify as home.

Zachary: *The Odyssey Project* unfolds as a class over six weeks. What are some things that happen during the six weeks that surprise you, even disappoint you, and challenge you?

Michael: The process is about defining the process as we're doing it rather than assuming we know everything going in. Every iteration is different. Even though I might have a sense of what might happen or what could happen, I have to be careful that it does not become "we should do this" or "this should happen." The process exposes the youth to this story, *The Odyssey*, and then they're asked to write in their words and through their lenses their biographical journey using *The Odyssey's* heroic template. The stories they create become the script.

They're also asked to draw pictures of various incidents, issues, and themes that *The Odyssey* sparks in their lives. And these drawings become the set. This phase goes along for three weeks, and at the end of that period, they have a script. Accomplishing a script in three weeks is ambitious, but that's the ideal. It doesn't always happen, and then we have to catch up in the remaining time.

In the second phase of the project, they learn and stage the script. At every point, there's a negotiation about who's the director, who's the author. The aim is to provide a space where the youth participants can take as much power as they need for their creative work. The disciplines leveraged are writing, drawing, animation, mask making, costume design, dance choreography, martial arts, rap, and other kinds of music composition.

The teaching artists come to the project bringing arts modalities and resources for the youth. Their professional expertise supports the youths' visions. The youth take over and determine what they want the outcome to be. This process culminates in a public performance that incarcerated peers attend if the facility allows them to come. We strive to invite people in power, lawmakers, and policymakers to make a difference in these youths' lives. The audience also includes family and friends who we hope will see the youth in a new positive light. We ask the university audience to view this project with an eye on community engagement. I must say the entire experience is a set of ongoing surprises, exhilarations, and challenges.

Zachary: Have you seen a shift in the relationship between the probation officers and administrators and the youth?

Michael: Yes. The work can sow seeds for change or hasten further growth in the seeds that are already planted. But I don't want to suggest that I go in there and magic happens. I have seen in the administrators and the probation officers who witness the work more acknowledging and concern for the youths' positive potentials, strivings, and struggles. They'll come up to the youth and say, "I didn't know you could rap, or I didn't know you could dance. I hadn't seen that side of you." I think there is a humanizing effect that fosters respect when this happens.

Zachary: If we were looking for that transformational experience, to view theater and creative arts as making an intervention into mass incarceration, what do you think it would require? What resources would you need, or would one need?

Michael: These words, *transformation* and *transformational*, have come under scrutiny (Nicholson, 2014, 15; Preston 2009; and Taylor 2003, 1–9). I use them carefully. I want to be careful about what I'm claiming. Transformation has metaphysical and spiritual connotations. In the work that I do, one might say, there is also a therapeutic connotation. However, I don't claim that this project can heal or transform. What I think is possible is for the process to provide a gearshift in the participant's awareness. There are lots of ingredients that pave the way for that shift, though. First, they have to want to change. They may not even fully know they want it, but something in the artistic activity can spark an awareness, and through that awareness, they get invested in wanting to change their lives or some part of their lives. However, they are really the activators.

The term intervention walks a thin line between words like invasion and intrusion (cf. Prentki 2009a). What makes an arts intervention successful is when it strikes a core of urgency coming from within the community. Interventions based on mutual agreement provide more motivated participation from people when they are stakeholders. As a teaching artist and facilitator, I'm always aware of my outside status (cf. Prentki 2009b, 252), no matter how much I relate to the population based on race, gender, class origins, or shared oppressions. Even if facilitators have authority as experts, the process has to be youth generated. Ultimately, the youth have to take it over. Six weeks is generally not enough time to allow transformation to happen. It can give participants a taste of that, and that taste can either be glorious or detrimental. It can be glorious, and it can hasten them to say, "I want to continue to do that, and I need to find a way. It's shifted my gears enough, and I see how the process connects to social, political, and personal things in my life, and I think I can make changes." Or it could be detrimental like a big opening but terrifying because they have to go back to a closed system, and they cannot quite make the connection between how work with *The Odyssey Project* reconciles with their life in prison.

It is essential to consider how their experiences with the project relate to life when they return home to an environment that has contributed to that person being who they are. It's a dance; it's a kind of maneuver, and I love those words – transformation, therapeutic, and intervention – but I also like to question them. "Intervention" means I'm coming in from the outside. I'm intervening because there is some problem. It puts me in a position of considerable authority. I think the key to effective artistic activism is that the facilitator has to listen.

Zachary: I think listening is intrinsic in your initial impulse because the class is called "The People's Voice," right? Is there something about allowing people to have their voice that is potentially liberating? And do you see their voice or voices, even if it's fleeting, emerging in the process?

Michael: When referring to voice in this work, I would say one can see tangible liberation if you will. Where I don't want to go is to say, "now I've transformed you, and you can go out into the world and live a wholesome life." Within the context of the project, people often open up and discover that using their voice is pleasurable; it's enjoyable – that their voice is powerful. And then by voice, I mean many avenues of voice. One could write, rap, move, dance, or draw.

Zachary: You are a teacher of voice. It seems like there are not only these different kinds of voice in terms of the practice but also a kind of political economy of voice(s) that the individual must negotiate. As a teacher of voice and vocal technique, what is your approach and training method with people rendered politically voiceless? Is there something that you hear? Is it a vibration?

Michael: Voice doesn't happen without breath. It is a complete way of opening up your reality. Once you're breathing and sound vibrations are travelling through your body, through your throat, into your face, and all over, then what happens? One feels more alive!

In my experience, with that aliveness comes vulnerability, and that's scary. Liberating the voice can lead to fear because then you feel what you've held in your body. There could be terrible memories that you've housed in your muscles and organs. Breathing is one way of experiencing whatever is in your being, and voicing stirs things up. In that release, there is often satisfaction. There's clearing. There is recognition, there's an acknowledgment that happens. These personal events inform the characters we play and are why voice work is so vital to the theater. But I don't think full-body breathing experiences should only be a privilege of theater people. It should also be a privilege of those who have been subsisting on minimal "what I need to survive" breathing. When people have access to their breath capacity in size and depth, it opens up all kinds of energy, and some of it is painful.

I don't deny that opportunity is there for people to face the fear. But it's important to prepare participants and set some terms of engagement. I talk to them about vulnerability because it's somewhat of a given in the theater, and most actors want access to their breath on those deep levels. They understand its importance, but when dealing with civilians, people who are not looking for a professional career in theater, vulnerability can threaten differently, holding the prospect of dismantling the survival armor that we need in the streets. The only argument I would have for taking that risk is that a voice is an essential part of their ability to express their feelings, thoughts, and personal power. And that expression goes towards defining and maybe even claiming what they want in life. That definition and claim should be established before engaging in creative tasks. Therefore, the facilitator strives to be transparent and engage the youth in honest discourse about how they see themselves and what goals they hope to achieve. I'll ask them, what do you want to get out of this project? What do you want to do with your life? How can the project bring you closer to what you indicated you want to achieve in life? They may not have all the answers, but the idea is to start thinking about the theater work that they're doing as a part of their life plan and the rehearsal space as a site for constructing their agency. Finding and refining self-determination are integral to the adventure of the voice. They're also determining what audience they want to reach. If they're going to be heard by certain people, then it becomes useful to be willing to breathe and to permit an opening to their experience that provides motivation and a focus for the messages they wish to convey.

In prison, facilitators must be aware of the ramifications of negotiating the terms of safe space and courageous space with the incarcerated.[1] Voice can open a gateway to courage, but we know that suppression of voice can be one intention of carceral space. Stimulating the voice with all of its biological, impulsive, intellectual, social, and political ramifications raises ethical questions about power. How dangerous, what consequences ensue from unleashing vocal power in a place of restraint? Is there defiance in this exercise of vocal power under these circumstances? In my experience, the youths' criticisms of the system have gone hand in hand with being held accountable for those expressions. The *Odyssey* may prime this balance as the hero continually reflects on his risky actions vs. the punishments of the gods. Incarcerated youth partaking in this project are writing their stories with a keen knowledge of detention. The activism of telling their stories in the place of confinement is a courageous act. Some risks of retaliation from the authorities in the system can be modified if the facilitator is aware of the injunctions against certain kinds of language and gang symbolism in their expressions. Still, the ethical issues that go with the tension between freedom and repression of the voice and the messages it carries in a place of detention need careful consideration by facilitators.

Zachary: You have done *The Odyssey Project* now at two different sites, first in Santa Barbara and now in Ventura. If you could have your dream for the future – all the resources that you could have – would that look like at a local, regional, and global level?

Michael: Ideally, *The Odyssey Project* would be part of a conversation integrated into penalty and rehabilitation institutions to support youth of color and offer options for them to review possibilities that would allow them to have fuller lives. Realistically, this project needs to happen in tandem with re-entry programs, programs that help people get jobs, get into colleges, or alternative training programs.

I see the problem that *The Odyssey Project* tackles as primarily a US problem because of our history of slavery and how we treat immigrants of color. Racism based on slavery is a hallmark of this country from its inception. It's harder for me to say globally. I'm looking at the US, and I hope this project would be useful to municipalities around the country. My vision would be for this to be part of a national conversation about the disproportionate incarceration of youth of color. To realize that, the project would need other facilitators, other people who want to do this kind of work in different regions of the country. I'm writing a manual that will provide a guide to the pedagogical process of *The Odyssey Project*. Again, I want to emphasize that I see the project as a component allied with other programs – so we're talking about re-entry, jobs, addiction services, treatment services, or whatever youth need as a part of the restorative process. The project works when the participants understand their worth and their sense of agency. But I believe humans are more successful in a society where they are cared for and valued and that leads to confronting the root issue, systemic racism.

Zachary: What advice would you offer others looking to develop pedagogical programs such as *The Odyssey Project*? Do you have suggestions for people who want to build programs that use either Classics or theater performance with incarcerated people? How would you advise that they start?

Michael: It always has to start with a compelling idea. From that idea, get alliances. You need to find a partner, and the first partner you need is a detention facility. Then conversations have to happen around schedules, agreements and funding. It's crucial to learn the ropes and learn the skeleton of your partner organizations. If you're working with detention, you don't have to become a lawyer or a criminologist. Still, you need to understand how those institutions work and know precisely what their mission statement is.

You can start with their website and learn who they are and what they want to do. So that there is a dovetail, and you can assure them that your project supports the work they are already doing if the facility states that their job is to educate and provide vocational services as the Department Description does for LPBC.[2]

Zachary: This sounds a lot like what performance studies ethnographers refer to as "co-performing" (Conquergood

2002). So, you really think that the process is about creating a community partnership?

Michael: You are working with organizations and often working for an organization. I work for a university. I'm juggling balls between two bureaucracies. You need to understand personalities and systems and how those organizations are structured to get things done and ensure your communications are transparent. With *The Odyssey Project*, I happen to be coming from a state-run institution. I'm dealing with a lot of state bureaucracy and red tape. Private schools may be different. Detention facilities are, by nature, organizational, hierarchical, and require a lot of structure because they predicate their entire order on safety. Detention facilities' state their primary mission is to protect the community. Tofteland discusses interfacing art with hierarchy and security in prisons (Tofteland 2011, 217–8). He points out it's important for a facilitator or project developer to understand the rules (cf. Tofteland 2011, 217–8) and to acknowledge that once you're entering that organization, you're a guest (cf. Prentki 2009b). You have certain guest privileges, but you're also an outsider and a visitor. It doesn't mean that you can't share experiences and be on some level equal. Perhaps you can seek that parity throughout the process, but in reality, you're not an inmate unless you consider yourself one in fellowship – sharing the bond of oppression. But there will always be a pragmatic distinction.

I would say build your idea out, so you're very clear about the concepts and the foundational principles guiding the work. This is a curriculum you're developing but be willing to be flexible in how you implement it because you want participation. These are participatory events. They have some theatrical elements in assigning roles of actor/writer/director, but as much as possible, one moves away from that model. We pull some methods and techniques from the theater, but the actual interactions should be collaborative. We know the theater is a collaborative art, but even within theater, there's a kind of reliance on hierarchy. But in an applied theater project, like *The Odyssey Project*, I would contest that model of traditional hierarchy placing the producer and director on top (cf. Prendergast and Saxton 2013, 6–7).

A curriculum needs flexibility, so you're not holding on tooth and nail. The idea is you're inviting people into this project to tell their stories, go on their journeys, and find themselves and their power. The process is about discovering identity and how they want to exercise their energies and creativity.

Notes

1 This was rightly emphasized by Joe Lambert in the oral presentation, titled "Facilitating a Story Circle: Goals and Guidelines," that he gave on August 12, 2019 in Berkeley, CA as part of the Facilitator's Workshop organized by StoryCenter.
2 Cf. https://www.countyofsb.org/ceo/asset.c/1755, accessed on December 5, 2020.

Works cited

Alexander, Michelle. 2012. *The New Jim Crow (Revised)*. New York: New Press.
Conquergood, Dwight. 2002. "Performance Studies: Interventions and Radical Research." *TDR (1988-)* 46 (2): 145–156.
Du Bois, W. E. B. 1989. *The Souls of Black Folk*. New York: Bantam Books. First published in 1903.
Freire, Paulo. 2000. *Pedagogy of the Oppressed*. New York: Bloomsbury Publishing.
Harney, Stefano, and Fred Moten. 2013. *The Undercommons: Fugitive Planning & Black Study*. https://www.minorcompositions.info/wp-content/uploads/2013/04/undercommons-web.pdf
Nicholson, Helen. 2014. *Applied Drama: The Gift of Theatre*. London: Palgrave Macmillan.
Prendergast, Monica, and Juliana Saxton. 2009. *Applied Theater: International Case Studies*. Bristol: Intellect.
Prendergast, Monica, and Juliana Saxton. 2013. *Applied Drama: A Facilitator's Handbook for Working in Community*. Chicago: University of Chicago Press.
Prentki, Tim. 2009a. "Introduction to Intervention." In *The Applied Theatre Reader*, edited by Tim Prentki and Sheila Preston, 181–183. New York: Routledge.
Prentki, Tim. 2009b. "Introduction to Border Crossing." In *The Applied Theatre Reader*, edited by Tim Prentki and Sheila Preston, 251–253. New York: Routledge.
Preston, Sheila. 2009. "Introduction to Transformation." In *The Applied Theatre Reader*, edited by Tim Prentki and Sheila Preston, 303–306. New York: Routledge.
Taylor, Philip. 2003. *Applied Theatre: Creating Transformative Encounters in the Community*. Portsmouth: Heinemann.
Tofteland, Curt L. 2011. "The Keeper of the Keys." In *Performing New Lives: Prison Theater*, edited by Jonathan Shailor, 213–230. London: Jessica Kingsley Publisher.
Wilderson, Frank. 2010. *Red, White & Black: Cinema and the Structure of U.S. Antagonisms*. Durham, NC: Duke University Press.

Part III

Critical pedagogy and the academy

9 Returning citizens and the responsibilities of the academy: teaching for Columbia university's justice-in-education initiative

Dan-el Padilla Peralta

Taking to heart the journalist and anthropologist Brian Goldstone's insistence that "ending the scourge of mass imprisonment must involve dismantling our degrading, dehumanizing narratives about both the innocent *and* the guilty" (Goldstone 2016), this chapter is grounded in a commitment to autobiographical narrative – and to the excavation of its underlying dehumanisms.

It was as a teenager that I went to Rikers Island for the first time, with my church youth group. The visits were arranged by Father Michael Sepp, then-pastor of Resurrection Roman Catholic Church in central Harlem. During those visits, usually scheduled for Lent and structured around a performance of the Stations of the Cross for our incarcerated community members, I shuttled between fear and anger.

The fear I resisted naming to myself, but its component features are not difficult to discern in retrospect. I was terrified of ending up on Rikers. My high school routines were studded with reminders of this statistical probability. The cops who walked me back to my Upper West Side private school in the belief that I was a truant, despite my protests that I had permission to leave my school building during free periods; the cops who knocked my apartment's door from its hinges in the mistaken belief that my home was a stash house for drugs; the cops who snatched up teenagers from the projects or the basketball courts, or traded fire with them in broad daylight or dead of night: "Man it's crazy and there's no escape/It's turned into a police state/The average cat don't even know his fate."[1]

The anger was a more complex emotion to parse. I perceived, dimly at first but later with blinding clarity, that among the enticements of my matriculation into the study of Classics was the fantasy of epistemic mastery over Whiteness.[2] Over and over again, my high school and college teachers sold me on the possibilities of mastery, especially in connection with language acquisition. Latin and ancient Greek were sites for the exercise of mastery; I could one day master them, provided I drilled and read and drilled and read. The drive to mastery, its psychic needs bearing down on me the more I took stock of the precarity that came with being an Afro-Latino undocumented immigrant, took its cue from the ruthless instruction in racialization at those predominantly White institutions where I came of age: "That sky was bluest when I could beat my mates at examination-time, or beat them at a foot-race, or even beat their stringy heads."[3] "With other black boys the strife was not so fiercely sunny" – that I knew; but with the drumbeat of mastery pulsing so loudly in my head I allowed myself little patience for my own mistakes, and no patience for what I took to be the mistakes of my Black and Latino peers. If they misstepped, if they could not walk on the straight and narrow path, that was *their* problem, or so I made myself believe.

I did not know what to do with my anger. Nor did I know what to do with another discovery, by turns provocative and unmooring, that sharpened the anger's edges: the revelation that indoctrination in mastery, along the axes plotted by the field to which I aspired one day to belong, left me no better positioned to understand the types of racial mastery that were exercised upon *me*. Nowhere in the field of Classics as it was being made apprehensible to me could I turn for an education in how and why I had become implicated in my own subjection. "Haunted and mad," I was nonetheless far from grasping the need to map "the trajectory of the racial, that modern signifier that delimits all the murders producing the *place* where the lives, the social trajectory, of racial subaltern projects unfold."[4] I was incapable of this act because I could not unthink my commitment to mastery; it simply was not conceivable to me that there were ways of living that strove conscientiously against mastery.[5] And I could not unthink mastery because I was afraid.

Some 15 years after my first visits to Rikers, I arrived on Columbia University's campus as a Mellon Research Fellow in the Society of Fellows. Two months after I started lecturing in the university's Core Curriculum, I was approached about the possibility of teaching in the Justice-in-Education Initiative, underwritten by a generous start-up grant from the Mellon Foundation.[6] The Initiative, a collaboration between the Society of Fellows and Heyman Center for the Humanities and the Center for Justice at Columbia, was conceived with several short- and long-term goals in mind: (1) "to offer courses, taught by Columbia instructors, in local prisons and to provide those who have come home from prison with the opportunity to continue their education at Columbia and its partner institutions, drawing on the support of community organizations"; (2) "to provide opportunities for jailed youth to engage with education"; (3) "to develop strong curricular support for the effective engagement of Columbia faculty and students in prison and jail education"; (4) "to change public and political thinking about the importance of access to higher education for the incarcerated and the formerly incarcerated"; and (5) "to not only make higher education available to a population that has been effectively excluded from it but also contribute to the growing movement to end mass incarceration."[7] The Principal Investigator for the Initiative was (and remains) Eileen Gillooly, Executive Director of the Heyman Center for the Humanities and Society of Fellows and Adjunct Associate Professor of English and Comparative Literature.

My motivations for joining the Initiative's work stemmed from two convictions. Rooted in the double consciousness that took shape around my experiences as an Afro-Latino undocumented immigrant was the realization that the carceral state and the immigration-enforcement state were two sides of the same coin.[8] Advocacy for immigration reform was steering me toward a reexamination of how I had entered the space of Classics, and emboldening me into adopting a more self-consciously activist praxis. Harnessing my own humanistic education as a resource for the pursuit of social justice seemed like the next logical step. I did not think that writing alone was enough: in the course of publishing a memoir that opened with a scene of police violence (Padilla Peralta 2015), I had become frustrated at the limitations of my own literary art when it came to rendering the carceral state's ubiquity during my childhood and adolescence.

But my main motivation for teaching within and against the prison–industrial complex snapped into focus during a presentation to Core Curriculum instructors in the fall of 2014. Slotted into the weekly line-up of the special lecture series for Core instructors was a panel presentation on contemporary social justice and mass incarceration, organized by Columbia's Center for Justice. The objective of this presentation was to model some effective strategies for opening up Core texts to discussions about racial and socioeconomic justice. For me, the intellectual and personal pleasures of this presentation quickly gave way to exasperation when a fellow Core instructor raised his hand to grumble during the Q&A: "I'm having a hard enough time getting my students to understand the basics of Plato and Aristotle.

How can I add all of this justice reform material?" Wedded to the idea that any discussion of contemporary justice reform was merely an add-on to the study of ancient and medieval philosophical texts, this instructor could not see his way to placing the twenty-first-century prison system in dialogue with Greek and Roman literature, even though this literature was obsessed with the theme of justice – and even though its conditions of production and circulation hinged on the profound injustices of slavery.

I did not trust myself to verbalize a response without yielding to the old anger. Two other Core instructors took the lead in vivisecting the grumble and proposing more pedagogically robust alternatives. But in the presentation's aftermath, I lingered long over the suddenness and intensity of my emotional response to my colleague's question. Having been repeatedly provoked and challenged by conversations with my own Core students about the explosive afterlives of the texts on our syllabus – it was the year of Ferguson – I was coming to terms with the notion that the oppressions of antiquity and modernity were in constant communication with each other, feeling my way toward a critical classical reception that took seriously the invitation to consider the field of my professionalization from the vantage of my immediate and embodied reception.[9] But this was slow and demanding work.

By the final stages of my doctoral training at Stanford University, I had realized that any program of research and publication that hewed closely to the traditional habits of scholarly detachment from the brute facts of structural oppression would deny me the opportunity to pursue that work much further. In the company of a close friend who taught under the auspices of the Prison University Project, I had visited San Quentin as a guest speaker for her Spanish 101 class; and I regularly corresponded with another close friend who had thrown himself into teaching history classes at San Quentin. But how much of that work was legible to or even valued by our academic mentors? Not much. And was it my sense of their resistance that had kept me from scaling up my commitment to teaching incarcerated scholars? No, I told myself, multiplying excuses; but in moments of genuine introspection I did not like the answer that arose from the depths of my professionalizing anxiety.

For a recently minted PhD in the midst of working through that anxiety, the Justice-in-Education Initiative offered a singular opportunity: to teach, on Columbia's Morningside Campus, a cohort of formerly incarcerated students in a skills-intensive course called "Humanities Texts, Critical Skills" that I would be permitted to design. It was agreed that the course would be co-taught, as a way to build up the roster of instructors and to expose the enrolled students to a variety of teaching styles. For the course's first iteration in the summer of 2015, my co-instructor Emily Hainze (PhD, English) and I settled on Homer's *Odyssey*, Sophocles' *Antigone*, Plato's *Lysis*, Books 8 and 9 of Aristotle's *Nicomachean Ethics*, Shakespeare's *Othello*, W. E. B. Du Bois' *The Souls of Black Folk*, and Tayeb Salih's *Season of Migration to the North*. The second iteration of the course was offered in the spring of 2016, a scheduling that enabled my co-instructor Anne Diebel (PhD, English) and me to take full advantage of a standard-length Columbia semester and to vary the original syllabus.[10] Following a two-semester hiatus, I returned to the J-i-E instructor ranks one final time in summer 2017, co-teaching with Nicole Callahan (PhD, English Education) a version of the 2015 syllabus that in-corporated Vladimir Nabokov's *Lolita* and Toni Morrison's *Song of Solomon*.

Organized as a two-hour seminar and heavy on animated discus-sion, the class met twice a week at night in order to accommodate returning citizens who worked during the day. To recruit students, Justice-in-Education worked with several institutions and organiza-tions, both at Columbia (the Center for Justice, Teachers' College) and beyond (Prison-to-College Pipeline, College and Community Fellowship, Correction Association of New York/Harlem Clemente Course, the Coming Home Program at Mount Sinai Hospital, the Racial Literacy Roundtable, The Precedential Group), to identify and nominate for enrollment in the course formerly incarcerated and re-cently returned citizens who had not completed their postsecondary education. Columbia tuition fees for the target number of nine en-rolled students were covered by J-i-E's Mellon grant, as were curri-cular and logistical supports: book purchases, transportation costs, and childcare. Students received Columbia email addresses and identification-card access to Columbia's Butler Library. The activation of these IDs, and in fact their official registration in the course, was conditional on their first submitting immunization records – a re-quirement, mandated by New York State law, that regularly posed an obstacle to students who did not have access to their immunization records, had never been vaccinated, or declined to be vaccinated on religious grounds. Upon successful completion of the course, each student received four Columbia credits, which they could apply toward a degree at Columbia or at another postsecondary institution.

For coordination of course logistics, registration, and continuing support for the Scholars, the Initiative tapped the services of two Program Managers: Christina Dawkins, who worked at the Initiative for the first year and a half of its implementation; and Richard Roderick, who stepped into the role after her departure. Their expertise and savvy in lining up resources for our students were vital in guaranteeing the Initiative's stability. In the inaugural cohort, six of the nine students who enrolled completed the course and received full credit. Of the three who were unable to complete the course, one had a probation officer who did not wish to cooperate with our student's desire to take a course that met at night, the second saw their summer upended by a major family medical emergency, and the third was forced to drop the course after the police arrested his teenage son. Seeing individual students continue in higher education, especially at Columbia – two J-i-E alumni were admitted to the School of General Studies, while another launched a new arts initiative in collaboration with the Center for Justice[11]– brought me a joy that was unlike anything I had ever felt before as an educator. But repetitive re-inscription into the rhythms of carcerality menaced the members of each cohort.

As for the mechanics of the course itself, setting realistic and attainable standards for reading and writing demanded both flexibility and improvisation. As co-instructors, we wanted to challenge, but not daunt; push, but not overwhelm. Originally, we envisioned four response papers and two short essays, but this arrangement rapidly ceded ground to the reality that, within each cohort, differences in age and educational attainment meant that levels of familiarity and comfort with college-level writing and reading varied widely. As my second semester of teaching HTCS drew to a close, it was obvious that more support structures for writing were needed, ideally in the form of writing tutors. The Initiative eventually secured the services of an undergraduate writing tutor, and the result was a measurable improvement in the quality and depth of student writing.

Where J-i-E made only limited progress, however, was in navigating the force-field of structural pressures that impinged substantially on the quality of life of formerly incarcerated adults. Here a tension rapidly opened up between the specific aims of HTCS as a course and the more encompassing vision of the Initiative as a whole. J-i-E extended far beyond the class: in addition to supporting teaching on the inside, the Initiative was also a gateway to transformative opportunities on and off Columbia's campus. Some of our scholars took the lead in organizing conferences and symposia,[12] which were integral not only to their formation as civically engaged members of the Columbia community but also to the world-building and networking that, in more than a few cases, opened doors to longer-term re-integration. Especially for those students who had only recently returned home, the temptation to overcommit was irresistible. They wanted fervently to restore and multiply those civic and cultural connections that the carceral state had taken away from them. They also wanted to maintain and amplify connections to those on the inside, and to ensure that the voices of those on the inside were heard on Columbia's campus. The pursuit of these connections, enriching and uplifting as they were, did not always leave time for a sustainable commitment to the course's demands. Even if, on an abstract level, I understood the importance of evading what Stefano Harney and Fred Moten have sparklingly described as the "call to order" – and the critical urgency of allowing our students the comfort and security to flee from my classroom in the search for their freedom – I had to unlearn my own disciplining within the academy in order to grant grace.[13]

For some students, balancing commitment to the course with yearning for contact and fulfillment outside of the classroom brought on stress and anxiety, in forms that the co-instructors were not always equipped or trained to handle. This observation brings me to the second, and major, challenge faced by the HTCS instructors: how to craft a classroom space that accommodated expressions of trauma and that was welcoming to traumatized students but did not seek to *exploit* that trauma in the service of pedagogy. From the work of socially engaged humanists in Classics and related fields,[14] I had gained some awareness of the importance of active listening. Inspired by the example of my co-instructors, I became more comfortable with modeling the kind of critical (and renegade) open-endedness that could inspire students to pursue therapeutic interpretations, at their own pace and inclination. But it was not until after my three-term stint that I became better attuned to and more fluent in trauma-informed pedagogy, thanks to works such as Becky Thompson's *Teaching with Tenderness: Toward an Embodied Practice* (2017). And it was not until my final term as a HTCS instructor that the Initiative set up a system for educating students about and guiding them to the mental health resources on Columbia's campus, and even then knowledge about access to these resources did not circulate to all of our students.[15] Those students who did make use of these resources remarked more than once that therapists primarily trained to counsel young adult undergraduates lacked the requisite skills for helping them manage their traumas.

Sometimes intentionally, but more often than not by felicitous accident, we built the practice of therapeutic interpretation into the writing prompts for the assigned essays and short responses, several of which tried to marry consideration of form – the epic simile in

Homer, the rhetoric of the Periclean Funeral Oration, the beat of Shakespearean verse – to a critical regard for literary representations of interiority. A student's searching meditation on the "humanizing moment of Hector smiling in silence at his infant son" in *Iliad* 6, and that speech to Andromache whose layers of psychological ambivalence reminded them "of the mentality of street gangs"; another student's flash of insight into Othello and Desdemona's biracial relationship, "which even to this day is perceived by some as taboo"; a peer's attention to the "poetic words" of *Lolita*'s Humbert Humbert, "deceiving readers of his revolting vice," and their classmate's sensitivity to the novel's insistence that we "pay attention to the style and structure of literature" and resist the encroachment of "the ism's that remain ever present in the world": these were high-water marks.

However, the main vehicle for therapeutic interpretation was seminar discussion, which for the first time in my teaching career came truly alive as a staging-ground for "relations of knowledge and the body," as knowledge was traced against the frontier of death.[16] The conversations flowed, on many days seemingly effortlessly, around and through the specter of the prison state. A week and a half into the inaugural offering of HTCS, a student began to draw parallels between the fantasy of Odysseus ever making it truly "home" and their own struggle to achieve homecoming in the face of structural and institutional barriers. Later that term, while wrestling with the *Nicomachean Ethics*, another student explained that, if friendships really did rest on reciprocity, they understood why their old friends had faded away when the student was on the inside; incarceration shut the door on the kinds of face-to-face and interpersonal reciprocity that had defined their group of friends, leaving only the monitored call or visit as pale substitutes. The second semester I taught HTCS, we were discussing the *Philoctetes* and the process of dissociating from one's physical pain when one student ventured their own recollection of traumatic dissociation: not long after being released from incarceration for the first time, they were in the midst of an outdoor drug sale that went sideways; the student ran and ran and ran; for the briefest moment, they thought they were in the clear – until they looked down at their arm and realized that it was riddled with bullets.

For me, these moments were ample vindication of James Baldwin's encomium to reading: "You think your pain, and your heartbreak, are unprecedented in the history of the world. But then you read" (Baldwin in Howard 1963). Our confidence in the course's strengths in design and execution received affirmation in several end-of-semester evaluations, most memorably in the words of the student who wrote:

"I was never expecting to feel the feelings I felt in this class. I was as lost as Odysseus, as manipulative as H. H., and as loving and caring as some of the gods toward my fellows." Yet the liberatory labor of reading and writing in community was hardly an unmitigated triumph.

My co-instructors and I were not always sufficiently thoughtful and responsible in introducing or framing those texts on the syllabus that could and did trigger our students. The decision to teach *Lolita* was especially fraught, and yielded starkly divergent outcomes the two times that we taught it. For the spring 2016 offering of HTCS, a student who listened to an audiobook version of *Lolita* found it to be uniquely resonant in cadence and content; they were a poet who, having composed chapbooks while on the inside, saw in *Lolita*'s lyricism a treasure-trove of imagery and language for representing and working through their own trauma. In the summer of 2017, however, one of our students began to sob as they discussed how harrowing it was for them to work through the novel without any guidance from the co-instructors on how to process the memories of sexual violence that came flooding back. I ultimately came to the conclusion that *Lolita*'s placement on the syllabus was too risky, at least until I deepened my own understanding of how better to support students whom the novel would re-traumatize.

In the midst of learning from our students which texts gave them the resources that they needed, I became more sensitive to the weight not only of their words but also of their bodies. The physical presence of our students on Columbia's campus, which has historically and to this day cordoned itself from the majority Black and Brown neighborhoods of upper Manhattan that are being swept up and away by the tides of university-fuelled gentrification,[17] was in itself a call to a new order. It became increasingly obvious to me that the vision of opening our texts to the readings that our students brought to the classroom had to proceed in conjunction with a more comprehensive program of human emancipation that razed campus gates and prison compounds. Indeed, the work of empowering the generations of J-i-E Scholars could not stop at skills-intensive humanistic training; it had to embrace a practice of world-building that extended to abolition.

In her response to Danielle Allen's Tanner Lectures (published in 2016 as *Education and Equality*), the playwright Quiara Alegría Hudes (2016, 97–8) reflected on the incarceration of her two young cousins, and on her desires for their liberation. "My deeply personal wish is for a humanities education that would teach my cousins to notice their automatized lives, to pay attention to that which has become so obvious as to seem unchangeable and inevitable, and to write it down … I want my cousins to have jobs, yes, absolutely, but I have a deeper ambition for them, one that includes and eclipses the marketplace: that my cousins not just be world inheritors but also become world builders." The single most extraordinary reward of J-i-E was to join the Scholars in their enterprise of world-building, and to be welcomed by them as a collaborator in that project. But standing in the way of that project's fruition are those institutions that, from the formative episodes of my childhood and adolescence to the very moment that I type these words, conditioned me into the uncritical endorsement of humanistic self-mastery as the ticket out of racial subjection. The humanities can be an effective armament for justice, but only to the extent that points of entry into their study are not monitored by those wardens intent on distinguishing the good Blacks from the bad.

Earlier I referred to empowerment. While access to the resources for world-building will empower J-i-E Scholars, my deeper ambition is for them to build a world that redistributes power to them. That redistribution would do more than simply increase their numbers at institutions of higher learning; it would abolish incarceration.

Notes

1 Beatnuts, "No Escapin' This" (*Take It or Squeeze It*, Loud Records, 2001).
2 Further on this point, and with reference to Chae 2018, see Padilla Peralta, in production.
3 This and the next sentence: Du Bois [1903] 1999, 10.
4 I follow but modify the structure of an important sentence in the conclusion to Ferreira da Silva 2007, 261.
5 For the concept of "unthinking mastery," see Singh 2018.
6 Announcement of the grant: http://heymancenter.org/public-humanities-initiative/phi-news/1-million-grant-awarded-from-andrew-w-mellon-found ation-for-new-justice-in/.
7 Full description of the Initiative's aims and objectives: http://justice ineducation.columbia.edu/about/overview/.
8 Gottschalk 2014, 215: "most discussions of the carceral state ignore how the line between immigration enforcement and law enforcement is rapidly disappearing in the US."
9 Critical classical reception: Hanink 2017.
10 It also enabled us to offer the course to Columbia undergraduates as well; two enrolled. But the move toward shaping HTCS into a course that brought together Columbia undergraduates and formerly incarcerated scholars into one community crystallized after my time teaching in the Initiative. Discussion of this move's pedagogical rewards and challenges: Callahan 2018.
11 The Confined Arts: https://www.theconfinedarts.org/our-team.html.
12 Among the best attended of these symposia were the multiple installments of The Confined Arts Initiative (see, e.g., http://justiceineducation.

columbia.edu/events/2016/03/12/the-confined-arts-solitary-confinement-edition/) and *Real Women, Real Voices* (http://justiceineducation.columbia.edu/events/2016/02/26/real-women-real-voices/).

13 The "call to order" and fugitive study: Harney and Moten 2013.
14 See, e.g., the essays in Rabinowitz and McHardy 2014.
15 This was confirmed by the comments of one student on their end-of-semester evaluation.
16 I am quoting and paraphrasing Barthes 1989, 338.
17 Contextualization of the Manhattanville construction project's residential impacts: Stewart 2019.

Works cited

Barthes, Roland. 1989. "To The Seminar." In R. Barthes, *The Rustle of Language*, 332–342. Translated by Richard Howard. Berkeley: University of California Press.

Callahan, Nicole. 2018. "Why We Must All Be Philosophers: Ethical Education and a Poetics of Freedom." *EuropeNow*, November 8, 2018. https://www.europenowjournal.org/2018/11/07/why-we-must-all-be-philosophers-ethical-education-and-a-poetics-of-freedom/.

Chae, Yung In. 2018. "White People Explain Classics to Us: Epistemic Injustice in the Everyday Experiences of Racial Minorities." *Eidolon*, February 5, 2018. https://eidolon.pub/white-people-explain-classics-to-us-50ecaef5511.

Du Bois, W.E.B. [1903] 1999. *The Souls of Black Folk*. Edited by Henry Louis Gates, Jr. and Terri Hume Oliver. New York: W.W. Norton.

Ferreira da Silva, Denise. 2007. *Toward a Global History of Race*. Minneapolis: University of Minnesota Press.

Goldstone, Brian. 2016. "Justice For All." *Jacobin*, April 8, 2016. https://www.jacobinmag.com/2016/04/kalief-browder-prison-reform-clinton-criminal-justice.

Gottschalk, Marie. 2014. *Caught: The Prison State and the Lockdown of American Politics*. Princeton: Princeton University Press.

Hanink, Johanna. 2017. "It's Time To Embrace Critical Classical Reception." *Eidolon*, May 1, 2017. https://eidolon.pub/its-time-to-embrace-critical-classical-reception-d3491a40eec3.

Harney, Stefano, and Fred Moten. 2013. *The Undercommons: Fugitive Planning and Black Study*. New York: Minor Compositions.

Howard, Jane. 1963. "Telling Talk From A Negro Writer." *Life*, May 24, 1963: 81–92.

Hudes, Quiara Alegría. 2016. "A World of Cousins." In Danielle Allen, *Education and Equality*, 89–98. Chicago: University of Chicago Press.

Padilla Peralta, Dan-el. 2015. *Undocumented: A Dominican Boy's Odyssey from a Homeless Shelter to the Ivy League*. New York: Penguin Press.

Padilla Peralta, Dan-el. In production. "Anti-Race and Anti-Racism: Whiteness and the Classical Imagination." In *A Cultural History of Race*. Vol. 1: *Antiquity*, edited by Denise McCoskey. London: Bloomsbury.

Rabinowitz, Nancy S., and Fiona McHardy, eds. 2014. *From Abortion to Pederasty: Addressing Difficult Topics in the Classics Classroom.* Columbus: Ohio State University Press.

Singh, Julietta. 2018. *Unthinking Mastery: Dehumanism and Decolonial Entanglements.* Durham: Duke University Press.

Stewart, Mariahs. 2019. "Private Universities Bring New Growth, But Gentrification Can Sideline Existing Residents." *Insight Into Diversity,* August 7, 2019: https://www.insightintodiversity.com/private-universities-bring-new-growth-but-gentrification-can-sideline-existing-residents/.

Thompson, Becky. 2017. *Teaching with Tenderness: Toward an Embodied Practice.* Urbana: University of Illinois Press.

10 Racing and gendering classical mythology in the incarcerated classroom

Elena Dugan and Mathura Umachandran

In Fall semester 2017, the co-authors of this paper (one a white American woman, one a non-Black British woman of color) taught a course with two other graduate students (both white men, neither of whom were American) at a maximum-security prison in New Jersey. Our classroom had roughly 25 students all of whom were men, both white and BIPOC, of a variety of ages above the New Jersey classification of "juvenile." The course was designed to run inside in parallel with an outside classroom, the latter in the elite university where the four instructors were all graduate students. In this piece, we reflect on the experience of teaching Classical Mythology as female instructors who are racialized as a white person and as a non-Black person of color, respectively. We will be forming our analysis through the overlapping lenses of class, race, and gender. For the sake of protecting our students' rights to confidentiality, we are choosing not to include identifying information about them.

We will reflect upon how in our course we attempted, with varying degrees of success, to de-center the exclusive focus on Greece and Rome with comparative material from the Ancient Near East and the Bible. We will also explore how the disciplinary insistence within Classics on expertise in the ancient languages allowed us to overlook linguistic expertise in the classroom, in a way that we recognize now is clearly inflected by race. Finally, we will examine how the tendency in Greek and Roman mythology towards representing misogyny and sexual violence presented particular challenges in the incarcerated classroom.

Thus, we intend not only to bring into focus how Classics is entangled with unjust gendered and racialized structures of power but also to examine what it would take to build a Classical Mythology course divested from these structures of power. What does an inclusive feminist and anti-racist Classical Mythology course look like, and where should it be taught? It is entirely possible that such a course could not take place, given the histories of social exclusion and injustice in which Classics has been implicated. We also feel, however, a cautious optimism, inspired by our students, that we might find more (if not perfectly) just ways forward.

Shaping the classical mythology syllabus for a parallel incarcerated course

The course was designed to introduce students to Classical Mythology. At least one person on the team had been an assistant instructor on the course as it was run at the university. The NJ-STEP program coordinated state-wide adult education in prisons: graduate student teachers would design syllabi and then submit these for approval to NJ-STEP and, through them, the accrediting institutions. Through taking approved courses, students could gain credit towards an associate- or bachelor-level degree. The syllabus for our course had further limitations because the accrediting institution, where the outside course was taught, had a say about what was taught. As far as possible, the parallel course was supposed to offer the same content with the same resources and assessments. The outside course that we were modeling involved twice-weekly lectures plus smaller discussion sections. As the inside instructors, we had to adjust our student-facing time to fit both lecture and discussion into twice-weekly two-hour blocks, with no possibility of contacting our students in the interim. A professor leading the outside course acted as a discretionary fifth member of our team, joining the teaching pair once every two weeks and providing extra support in optional "tutoring" sessions.

"White man's mythology": putting Greece and Rome into comparison

Across Classics in the last few decades, various strategies have put the Greeks and Romans into the context of a broader ancient world. For example, ancient historians have undertaken comparative empire studies or post-colonial critiques of Athenian and Roman imperial networks, while historians of medicine have investigated the production of knowledge across and beyond the Mediterranean (cf., e.g., Zucconi 2019). Not all scholars who do this work necessarily see expanding the geographical referents of antiquity beyond Greece and

Rome as a political project. However, we were keen not to limit our material to Greco-Roman thought and thereby reaffirm triumphalist ideas about "Western civilization" in Classical Mythology.

Our teaching team included a graduate student in the Religion department working on apocryphal ancient Jewish, Christian, and Islamic texts, and a historian of philosophy working on the cultural connections between Greece and the ancient Near East in pre-Socratic thought. In the sessions run by the Near-Eastern specialists, we opened up comparative perspectives, assigning Hesiod's *Works and Days* alongside Akkadian and Hebrew Biblical material to support discussions of the source of myth, especially in contexts geographically and culturally proximate to Hesiod himself. We wanted to acknowledge that there are many mythological texts and stories worthy of study – none of us wanted to teach a course that reproduced "the Greek miracle."

Many students entered the classroom with particular investments in antiquity. For example, students who identified as Christian and Muslim had personal and intellectual interests in the ancient texts produced and valued by their given traditions, and the contexts which produced them. Thus, we could count on certain subsets of students perking up when presented with, for instance, the Qur'anic account of the Flood alongside Ovid's *Metamorphoses*, perhaps thanks to the joys of recognizing something that was "theirs" alongside the classical material that was "ours." However, these moments of recognition were problematic. In this classroom, all of our Muslim students also identified as Black.[1] No member of the teaching team, text, or author on the syllabus shared this conjunction of race and faith in their identity. In providing Islamic texts as comparanda to the Greco-Roman backbone of the course, were we reaffirming the sense that these students could not find themselves reflected in the core material?

We were reminded that our students felt racialized exclusions acutely. At the end of our first class, a student whom we came to understand as the "grandfather of the house" (someone with seniority within the wider social life of the prison) raised his hand and asked: "Isn't this all white man's mythology?" He rightly questioned our teaching *this* course in *this* classroom. Our students were articulate around questions of race, and were not afraid to give voice to them. Part of our job became facilitating the critical discussion of Classical Mythology when it was *and was perceived as* part of the violent apparatus of white supremacy within an incarcerating institution. One of the stated course goals was to provide: "a stimulus for thinking about the role of mythology today, and the way that we use stories to understand ourselves and our world." The grandfather of the house had already reflected extensively on Classical Mythology in understanding his place in the world, long before we had walked into the classroom.

We came to realize that the advantage of a comparative curriculum was our students' formulation of questions shaped by their own religious and cultural traditions. They investigated our syllabus with questions such as: "What are myths, and where do they come from?"; "Where is the line between myth and scripture, if there is one at all?"; "Who wrote and transmitted ancient texts?"; "Why do ancient texts matter in the modern world?" Making space for such questions was a form of pedagogical re-centering. While this strategy did not resolve the alienation that many of our students felt, it allowed us to make space for engagement with the ancient material on terms closer to their own.

In many ways, these are the general benefits of a comparative curriculum that might be experienced in both outside and inside classrooms. Incarceration, however, brought certain aspects of our students' identities to the fore (whilst taking away many other key parts of identity). Many of them, for example, indicated that their religious identities had taken on heightened importance during their incarceration. Points of intersection between the *realia* of their traditions and the syllabus seemed more immediately relevant to them than they might have outside the carceral walls. We came to realize, moreover, that their independent religious praxis was highly textualized: nearly all of our religious students participated in some sort of voluntary scriptural study, such as Bible or Qur'an study groups. Granted, the predominance of textual study among our students is one enforced by the confines of carceral facilities, which constrain freedoms of movement, speech, and action that are the conditions for the possibility of other religious praxes. Nevertheless, religious identities and praxes became a formative influence on our classroom dynamic. The stimulating discussions we enjoyed when integrating non-classical textual material, especially from religious traditions with modern adherents, encouraged us to keep it up over the course of the semester.

The limitations of time and space, however, impinged on how far we could deconstruct normative ideas of the "classical." Our main directive was to teach Classical Mythology, even when this objective was at odds with the core learning objectives of our diverse student body, as was often implied and sometimes explicitly stated by our students.

Competency and exclusions: the politics of language

At the start of the course, we distributed a survey to gauge our students' interests, education, and competencies. We also asked about linguistic background, expecting that a number of our students would name Spanish as their first language, given that the US disproportionately incarcerates people of color, including Latinx populations. But the linguistic competencies that our students initially disclosed, and those which we later discovered, unmasked the exclusionary logic of linguistic competency underlying Classics.

In response to the survey, some students named Ebonics or African American Vernacular English (AAVE) as their primary or secondary language competency. Borne out of the conditions of slavery in the American South, AAVE is a mode of communication that resists and circumvents power structures that enforce whiteness. While it has complex grammatical structures and dialect variations, it has been situated overwhelmingly as non-standard English and therefore as an incorrect or defective means of communication (Hobbes 2017). AAVE has had limited formal recognition within the American education system, and has only recently been recognized by socio-linguists as worthy of academic study. As a result of historically institutionalized racism, then, the insistence on "standard" English as the default language in which (most) educational institutions operate might appear as neutral, but in fact it delegitimizes discourses, including AAVE, that fall beyond that narrowly defined standard. From the outset then, we risked compounding the dehumanizing effects of incarcerated spaces by replicating the exclusionary language practices of most traditional classrooms.

As we got to know our students, we realized that the survey had given us a partial image of the classroom. One student informed us on the survey that he wanted to go to Bible college, and only later told us he was therefore learning New Testament Greek in his spare time. Other students were studying Qur'anic Arabic, but did not see this as a relevant disclosure. In understanding that particular kinds of answers were withheld, we were forced to confront how language competency operates in our professional formation. Classics requires mastery not only over ancient languages (Greek and Latin) but also over a number of European languages (most commonly German, French, Italian). Moreover, language competency keeps together the various subdisciplines under the big tent of Classics, and thus there is an impetus to use language competency as a tool of gate-keeping as much as disciplinary cohesion. In failing to encourage our students to disclose their expertise in ancient and medieval languages other than Greek and Latin, we silently confirmed what they already suspected: that Classics addresses itself to a narrow subsection of European culture and history, and goes out of its way to underscore the exceptional value of its objects, thus rendering knowledge about other parts of the world irrelevant.

Teaching Ovid's rapes

Our bright students brought energy and dedication to the course despite the challenges of living in a profoundly dehumanizing place. The rape and misogyny narratives that occur frequently in classical myths, however, marked one of the most challenging aspects of teaching this course. Our syllabus did not reserve a particular week for gender or gendered violence as such. However, the abuse of power in the relationships between gods and humans is hard to miss in Greco-Roman mythological narratives, as are the ways in which that power is gendered so that male gods often use it over mortal women as rape. Beyond the frequent representations of gendered violence, women are conspicuously stigmatized in this body of literature.

Gender was brought into focus early on in the organization of the course: part of Prometheus' challenge to Zeus' domination is the creation of Pandora and woman, according to Hesiod. The insistence that the creation of women was concomitant with mortal sin led us into discussions of gender relations as represented in Greek mythology. We assigned the viciously misogynistic texts by Semonides and his typology of animal comparisons, as well as Euripides' *Hippolytus* with its sex-phobic main character. Reactions from students to these texts ranged from surprise in seeing contemporary attitudes voiced in ancient texts, disgust for the lack of respect expressed, or amusement at (for example) Semonides' comparisons. We were able to touch briefly on masculinity in our mid-term discussions about the nature of Heracles' heroism, discussions in which our students explored the relationship of masculinity to violence especially in systems of control that promote violence such as Zeus'. This laid the groundwork for moving into discussions of Ovid.

Other Classicists have addressed how painful it is to be in classrooms where sexual violence as represented in ancient poetry is mishandled and discussed as separate from the experience of those living within the broad spectrum of sexual violence (from harassment to rape) as a structuring part of their lives (Beek 2016). This issue has predominantly been raised by female Classicists, but, of course, it affects male and non-binary scholars and students of the ancient world too. In including works by Ovid and Semonides on our syllabus, we were aiming to face the literary evidence from the ancient world head-on without damning it totally either.

How, then, to deal responsibly with the mythological aspects of sexual violence, when we had no formal counseling training in these areas? This is a particularly urgent question in the incarcerated classroom, since our students were drawn from a population that inhabit their own complicated set of positionalities with respect to sexual violence, not least that they themselves are disproportionately vulnerable to it. As Maurice Chammah (2015) observes, the 2003 Prison Rape Elimination Act "was intended to make experiences (of sexual violence) far less likely. But like many ambitious pieces of legislation, its promise has proved difficult to realize." Moreover, in the maximum-security setting, our classroom may well have held students convicted (whether rightly or wrongly) for committing this violence, or who having committed this violence, find it abhorrent now.

We did not have much time to examine the historical status of women in archaic and classical Greece and Rome, or to explore how the mythological framework did or did not map onto socio-cultural development. Nor do these texts themselves automatically bring students to think through such lenses. For instance, the rape of Persephone by Hades in Ovid's *Metamorphoses* comes with no accompanying condemnation in the text. Our students, given the floor to share their observations on this portion of the text, brought out a rich and multifaceted set of perspectives on the themes, language, and poetry of the episode, none of which touched on sexual violence. At the end of this student-led discussion, it fell to one of the instructors to execute a sharp last-minute turn and flag the rape implied therein. Though a necessary and important feature of the story, the fact that its disclosure felt so awkward at the time (our talkative students fell silent near-immediately) reflects the inherent clash between the ways we teach students to parse carefully and take delight in classical myths, and the ways that classical myths crash not-so-carefully into modern feminist readings.

This led to deeply uncomfortable experiences for us, and for our students. Part of the discomfort we experienced was a general one with the material itself – for instance, with the explicit nature of the descriptions of rape in the *Metamorphoses* and with the apparent lack of retributive or reparative readings for some of these stories, especially that of Philomela. But part of our individual discomfort came from the interaction between our gender identities and our students'; being a female instructor in front of an all-male classroom is a situation rarely replicated in outside college classrooms. And, as the schedule worked out, it happened to be that the two female instructors taught the most explicitly gendered violent content. We found ourselves on the spot – for even when as educators we have the most critical lens in mind, when standing in front of a classroom, we signal to our students that this material is worth paying attention to and invite their hearty engagement.

So, when close-reading Semonides, we were taken aback by students who took a "yes-and" attitude to his catalogue of reasons to despise women. We came to realize that the skill of close-reading, which we listed as one of the core course-objectives, tested for in nearly all of our assessments, and which we devoted many class periods to training and developing, encourages students to try their hardest to enter into the structures, worldview, and contours of the text. For students just learning this skill-set, the next implied skill, the pivot towards thinking critically about the observations made during close-reading, might not happen instantaneously. And so, we found ourselves with students doing exactly what we had asked them to do – entering into the world of classical myths, and repeating back the attitudes found therein. If we had done our jobs right, and gotten students passionate about the material, these observations would be communicated with excitement and vigor. It would then be our task to move students from the initial observational phase (in one memorable comment: "Semonides agrees with me, women never stop talking!"), to critical reflections on what they had excavated from the text, an exceedingly awkward maneuver for a female instructor to ask an all-male classroom to make, and one that we did not always execute successfully.

In the process of assessment, we had difficulty grading student engagement and written work that replicated the misogyny of the texts. The challenge of assessing work that is ideologically repellent but technically competent presents itself in outside classrooms as much as inside ones. Here, we also weighed larger structural questions. Was it not strange to ask incarcerated individuals to detach selectively from the carceral environment – from the racism, classism, sexism, and wholesale dehumanization with which the state violently structures our students' daily lives – just to spout a progressive line on gender or sexual violence for an essay? Our first instinct was to celebrate intellectual work that approximated feminist thinking, and condemn those that missed the mark. But we, as non-incarcerated women, are not subject to the kinds of violence our students were and therefore have the opportunity to imagine and practice different kinds of feminist worlds than our students. And yet we went into the practice of assessment expecting incarcerated men to produce work predominantly shaped by *our* intellectual world. This says more about our falling short of understanding the place of education within the system of incarceration than any failure on our students' part to critique misogyny sufficiently.

Conclusion

Classics has held an esteemed place in humanistic projects that emphasize the emancipatory value of education. By this logic, it should follow that an incarcerated classroom is an ideal venue to give people the chance to develop tools for greater human understanding by studying Classical Mythology. And yet, our experiences have shown us that Classics does not neatly line up with a pedagogical praxis of liberation. Rather, we recognize that we have been trained in ways that compounded some of the inequalities we were seeking to undo. We are still not sure if Classics education in incarcerated classrooms inherently possesses a credible best practice that we might have better emulated.

We replicated parts of exclusionary and supremacist structures of knowledge and experience despite our attempts at crafting a comparative and inclusive curriculum. But perhaps this is inevitable when teaching such an historically elite and exclusively defined discipline in classrooms peopled by those society has located outside its elite by virtue of race and/or class, not to mention their current status of incarceration. It was hard to be in solidarity with our students when they rightly called out the racialized supremacy of the subject matter. After all, we were the pedagogues who devoted so much effort to bring it to them. No matter our attempts at empathy and solidarity, were we not automatically proponents of the subject of our class?

This ambivalence was compounded for those of us on the teaching team who live at the intersections of oppression themselves. So, as female instructors, we found it difficult to be in solidarity with our students when they internalized and re-presented the misogynistic viewpoints in the texts of the course. For the female instructor of color, it was still more complicated to have her authority around this set of knowledge challenged by students. She appeared at the front of the classroom as the least likely person on the teaching team to hold expertise, and thus was exposed to students' various frustrations with the mythological material in ways that the white men and women teachers were not. The friction here was around authority itself, that is, the complex racialized and gendered ways in which oppression works to put students and teachers into relationships of antagonism rather than solidarity. When one of our students attached photocopies of Paulo Freire's *Pedagogy of the Oppressed* (1968) to his course evaluation forms rather than filling the forms in, he pointedly reminded us that pedagogical practices exist that resist authority altogether. That he had managed to get photocopies made inside the prison demonstrated his resourcefulness; that he undertook the equivalent of "spoiling his ballot" prompted us to reflect on our activity within institutions and unequal power structures, whether academia, the prison, or both.

In this piece, we have tried to reflect critically on our contributions to the interlocking logics of incarceration, white supremacy, and patriarchy. We both still find ourselves captivated by the passion, energy, and brilliance that our students demonstrated in conversation with Classical Mythology. We want to acknowledge, however, the ways in which Classics curricula in incarcerated classrooms uniquely implicate teachers and students in difficult ethical predicaments. We insist that this places an onus upon teachers to think critically about the material they bring inside.

In our particular case, given our teaching team and student roster, we faced up to difficult questions concerning race and gender, some of which we have tried to address in this essay. Other demographic configurations might bring different issues to the fore: in settings where average reading levels or English competency were far lower than our highly selective classroom, we can imagine a confrontation between the hyper-literate expectations of a Classics syllabus, the educational deficits faced by many incarcerated individuals, and the structures of social inequality that construe poverty and illiteracy as a racialized phenomenon.

Our view is that some kind of collision between Classics and the incarcerated classroom is inevitable. Should we consider the fallout a sign of the generativity of Classics on the inside? Or are we grappling with a troubling set of contradictions that are inherent in Classics and are brought into sharp definition by the paradoxical attempt to teach Classical Mythology within the dehumanizing institution of incarceration? We leave these questions open to discussion as we struggle together towards collective liberation.

Note

1 There is a long history connecting the struggle for prisoners' rights, the prison abolition movement, and Black prisoners' conversion to Islam. See Colley 2014, 393–415.

Works cited

Beek, A. Everett. 2016. "Ovid's Afterlife: Mythical Rape and Rape Myths." *Eidolon*, April 26, 2016, https://eidolon.pub/ovid-s-afterlife-4f708df9d244.

Chammah, Maurice. 2015. "Rape in the American Prison." *The Atlantic*, February 25, 2015, https://www.theatlantic.com/politics/archive/2015/02/rape-in-the-american-prison/385550/.

Colley, Zoe. 2014. "'All America Is a Prison': The Nation of Islam and the Politicization of African American Prisoners, 1955–1965." *Journal of American Studies* 48, No. 2 (May): 393–415.

Freire, Paulo. 2018. *Pedagogy of the Oppressed, 50th Anniversary Edition*. London: Bloomsbury Academic.

Hobbes, Michael. 2017. "Why America Needs Ebonics Now." *Huffington Post*, September 25, 2017, https://highline.huffingtonpost.com/articles/en/ebonics/.

Zucconi, Laura. 2019. *Ancient Medicine: From Mesopotamia to Rome*. Grand Rapids, MI: Eerdmans Publishing.

11 Critical perspectives on prison pedagogy and classics[*]

Jessica Wright

Prison education programs are an increasingly visible mode of social justice work across the academy, in Classics as in other disciplines.[1] By creating spaces for higher education within carceral institutions, humanities professors work to crack the walls of exclusivity and tradition that guard our fields, to unsettle the school-to-prison pipeline, to build bridges between "outside" (free-world) and "inside" (incarcerated) participants, and to provide intellectual, imaginative, and ethical resources for those who are locked up.[2] Prison education is often envisioned as liberatory, although many prison educators also recognize their implication in the mechanisms that sustain the carceral state. This tension, which Lori Gruen describes as one of the "vexations" of prison education, has produced abundant scholarship that reckons with the question of who and what prison education programs are for, and how they can be implemented without unwittingly exploiting incarcerated participants.[3] As Erin Castro (nonincarcerated instructor) and Michael Brawn (incarcerated student) have written, "The prison classroom is ultimately an extension of the carceral state, and this awareness should anchor an emplaced critical praxis in prison – an awareness to work against systemic state violence in such a way that honors the lived realities of imprisoned students" (Castro and Brawn 2017, 118).

For Classicists who teach in prisons as a strategy toward social justice, the tension between collaboration with and resistance to the carceral system is compounded by the historical and contemporary

* The reflections presented here were shaped by many generous and challenging conversation partners, including especially Shelley Haley, Nancy S. Rabinowitz, Mathura Umachandran, and Mel Webb. All errors of argument and thinking are, naturally, my own.

appropriation of classical antiquity to support imperialist and white supremacist ideologies. With its historical emphasis on the exceptionalism of Greece and Rome as the ancestral heritage of white Europeans, Classics has served as a tool for colonization (Goff 2005; Greenwood 2010; Haley 1993; Vasunia 2013). As such, it is a rich site for certain forms of decolonizing work (Ram-Prasad 2019; Umachandran 2019). At the same time, the capacity and desire to perform that work is constrained by the fact that Classics itself – like the humanities at large – is often seen to be under attack, marginalized, and forgotten. The tension between Classics as colonial tool and Classics as romanticized site of erasure makes social justice work within the field a challenge. Teaching Classics in prison can serve as much to buttress tradition as to redistribute intellectual capital.

During the second semester that I taught Latin through the Prison Teaching Initiative at Princeton University, I was approached by the director of an educational non-profit devoted to Classics and invited to collaborate with him to introduce Latin into every prison in North America. This was part of a broader scheme to demonstrate the importance of Latin to human intelligence: the hope was that, with time, compulsory Latin education would be re-introduced into the public education system. Projects such as this highlight the potential for instrumentalizing incarcerated participants in prison education programs. They prompt the questions: Who (or what) is prison education for? To what extent do Classicists who teach in prisons depend upon the labor of incarcerated students to make the politics of doing Classics more acceptable within a cultural moment defined by critiques of white supremacism? How can we teach Classics in prisons without instrumentalizing our students toward the renewal of our discipline?

In order to use prison education effectively as a tool for social justice, we must develop collective practices of critical reflection upon our prison pedagogies and programs, particularly with regard to their investment in classical antiquity. Here, I suggest resources for this project. I begin by laying out some of the debates in the field of higher education in prisons. My purpose is to situate the work of Classicists who teach in prisons, and the challenges we face, within the context of prison education more broadly.

Prison education as a tool for social justice: strategies and critiques

In 1994, when incarcerated students were excluded from receiving federal Pell Grants, many college-in-prison programs closed down due to lack of funding (Karpowitz 2017, 6–7). The programs that replaced these earlier initiatives typically were based in private institutions, and were either self-funded or supported by philanthropic grants. Many were run by volunteers, transforming prison education into a site for private philanthropy, volunteerism, and community service. These programs have come into the spotlight in recent years, in part because of the rising prominence of mass incarceration more generally. There are three common narratives through which such prison education programs are pitched to stakeholders, such as university deans and granting agencies.

First, access to higher education in prison reduces the rate of recidivism (Karpowitz 2017, 1–2, 33–5; Stern, 2014, 160–1). Prison educators have argued against the validity of this argument, although often they agree on its utility (Castro and Gould 2018, 5; Corbett 2018; Scott 2018, 3).[4] From a methodological vantage point, the unreliability of data collection methods and the lack of consensus regarding appropriate recidivism metrics makes the reduction of recidivism a weak motivation for creating educational opportunities (Scott 2018). Further, the emphasis on recidivism within research on prison education puts the burden on individuals to avoid re-incarceration, and, as such, circumvents structural analysis (Corbett 2018). From a political standpoint, arguments that "prioritize reduced recidivism" contribute to the commodification of education that is taking place on traditional college campuses and obscure the necessity for institutions of higher education to reflect on their "societal responsibility and opportunity ... during an era of mass confinement" (Castro and Gould 2018, 5). Kaia Stern (2014) makes a similar case from a theological perspective, drawing on the voices of incarcerated men to argue that mass incarceration in America is the consequence of a culture of punishment, and that it is the responsibility of all individuals to work toward fixing it. Arguments that focus on prison education as the means of alleviating mass incarceration, while useful in securing institutional funding and support, divert attention away from societal responsibility and place the burden of decarceration on the shoulders of incarcerated individuals, as though the structural problems that funnelled them into carceral spaces can be resolved by their own self-optimization.

A second strategy for authorizing prison education programs is to emphasize humanization, liberation, and empowerment. Scott concludes his critique of the "recidivism argument" by noting that prisons are "campuses of dehumanization," and that prison educators are motivated by the desire to reduce recidivism because they want to help "their students get out and stay out" (Scott 2018, 13). Lori Pompa, founder of the Inside-Out model of prison education, argues that higher education in prison "provides a space of liberation, a place in which each person is afforded dignity and recognized for the unique contribution that he or she brings to the whole" (Pompa 2013, 133). There are risks in these arguments also, in particular the dilution of the concept of freedom, which prison educators can share with incarcerated students only in symbolic form: "There is a common theme among some prisoners which states: though my body is incarcerated, my mind is free. I held that sentiment myself until I came to recognize that freedom is not so easily gained. The idea of freedom, what it means to be free, is complicated by experience. I am not free simply because I believe that I am" (Davis III 2018, 2). Emphasizing the liberatory or empowering potential of education in prison can obscure the material fact that nonincarcerated instructors leave the prison at the end of each class session, while incarcerated participants do not. Obscuring this difference can, in turn, serve to mystify the power relations between instructors and participants (Castro and Brawn 2017).

A third argument to support prison education initiatives is the impact they can have on nonincarcerated participants. In her reflection on the development of the Inside-Out program, Pompa notes that visiting prisons as educators and students can be educational and life-altering, arguing that through exchange, prison walls "will become increasingly permeable and, eventually, extinct – one idea, one person, one brick at a time" (Pompa 2013, 133). These claims are subject to the same challenge as arguments about intellectual liberation: the forms of imprisonment experienced by nonincarcerated instructors are qualitatively different to those of incarcerated students. In addition, emphasizing or prioritizing the benefits to nonincarcerated participants risks establishing a form of "academic tourism" that perpetuates the exploitation of incarcerated participants (Castro and Gould 2018, 6–8).

Prison educators, then, may unintentionally reinforce the hierarchies of the prison system. One counter-strategy is to avoid patronizing incarcerated students by setting high intellectual standards. Another is to employ critical pedagogy, which redefines the purpose of education as epistemological liberation through dialogue that presupposes instructor/ student equality. These approaches are not mutually exclusive, but as liberatory strategies they are in opposition: on the one hand, the traditional markers of academic success are protected in order to confer cultural capital upon incarcerated graduates; on the other hand, traditional academic practices are recognized as complicit in the authoritarian hierarchies that structure prison spaces, as well as in epistemological colonization (on this concept, see Hall and Tandon 2017).

Critical pedagogy, based on the work of Paolo Freire and bell hooks, is a prominent tool for working toward liberatory educational practices within prison classrooms (Freire 1968; hooks 1994). As hooks describes, "there are some classrooms in which individual professors aim to educate as the practice of freedom," through a student-centered pedagogy that "aims to restore students' will to think, and their will to be fully self-actualized" (hooks 2010, 8). These classrooms function "more like cooperatives," with the professor assuming a collaborative rather than authoritative position (hooks 2010, 22). As applied within the prison context, however, critical pedagogy can again mystify the institutionalized hierarchy between instructor and student, particularly since incarcerated students often rely entirely on sources provided by their instructors: "Personal, political, and philosophical commitments notwithstanding, nonincarcerated instructors who teach inside prisons and subscribe to critical pedagogy may run the risk of reproducing the very power structures they seek to expose by neglecting to consider incarcerated students' unique positionalities – specifically, their inability to access information freely and to exist in the world as independent thinkers" (Castro and Brawn 2017, 103).[5] It is necessary, when applying the methods of critical pedagogy, to acknowledge and address the inherent limitations of the carceral context.

Daniel Karpowitz, who serves as director of the Bard Prison Initiative, distinguishes three narratives that motivate prison education: (1) prison education reduces recidivism (instrumentalism); (2) prison education has liberatory potential (romanticism); (3) prison classrooms hold potential for restoring the humanist classics to the center of intellectual activity (conservativism) (Karpowitz 2017, 11). We have already explored the first two narratives. Here, I want to consider the third. Classical literature, especially epic and tragedy, is a powerful tool in prison classrooms, as in other sites of arts-based restorative and therapeutic work.[6] Yet, if Karpowitz is right, and the restoration of "humanist classics" to some extent motivates prison education programs, then we must engage in rigorous self-critique, especially since incarcerated students are inherently vulnerable. For what purpose are we teaching classical texts in prisons? For whom? Centering our incarcerated students, rather than classical texts, should be a constant practice, in order to ensure that we can resist the pull that "imperialist capitalist white-supremacist patriarchal politics" have exerted on "learning communities" throughout American history (hooks 2010, 29).

The purpose and motivations of prison education have become the site of heated debate. These debates matter because the narratives that nonincarcerated prison educators create about prison education can, regardless of intentions, reproduce carceral power structures. Self-reflexivity and mutual accountability are required in order to navigate the ethical ambiguities of prison education work. In what follows, I lay out some strategies for how we might cultivate these practices as a community of Classicists engaged in the work of prison education toward social justice.

Self-reflexivity and mutual accountability in classics-based prison education

First, it is vital to step out of the echo chamber of Classics itself.[7] The debates about how prison education should be conducted are vigorous. It is essential for Classicists to enter into these conversations. For example, we might consult with the Jamii Sisterhood (https:// jamiisisterhood.com), join the Higher Education in Prison Listserv (run by the Alliance for Higher Education in Prison: http://www. higheredinprison.org), or attend the National Conference on Higher Education in Prison. We must read widely in the scholarly literature on prison education in order to inform ourselves with regard to best practices. At a minimum, we should familiarize ourselves with *Equity and Excellence in Practice: A Guide for Higher Education in Prison* (Erzen, Gould, and Lewen 2019). As a community, we should develop a shared bibliography and crowdsource a list of experienced prison educators from other disciplines to invite into our workshops and conversations.

We also need to reflect on the imperialist, racist, and misogynist legacies and potential of our field – an area of research that has flourished in recent decades.[8] What do feminist, anti-racist, and anti-imperialist critiques of Classics look like in a prison context? How can we build a set of best practices for using Classics as a tool for transformative education in prisons? One strategy is to practice openness with our incarcerated students about the work that we do – and that very much remains to be done – to disentangle Classics from whiteness and coloniality (Wright 2017). This might be fruitful ground for conversation with prison educators in disciplines facing similar challenges, such as medieval studies. We must further collaborate with incarcerated students and program alumni in the development of syllabi and curricula. If our goal is to empower our students, then we must share power in decision-making and in speaking (hooks 2010, 22). Further, we must enable contributions by incarcerated students in our discussions of prison education. This practice of foregrounding the voices of incarcerated students is imperative if we are to avoid reinforcing structural hierarchies, and the results of this work can be rich (see, for example, Castro and Brawn 2017).

Finally, we must articulate our motivations in prison education. Clearly, these will not be uniform, and it is not my intention to suggest that they should be. It is necessary, however, to be transparent about who benefits from our work, and how. More precisely, we must ask not only how our incarcerated students benefit but also: How do we benefit from providing prison education? How do our departments and institutions benefit? What about the field of Classics as a whole? Further, what are the benefits to the Department of Corrections and the prisons or jails where we work?

Prison education is a site for doubling down on the value of the humanities. This is because of the heightened instrumentalization of education within carceral spaces (prison education is justified in terms of its effects after re-entry, whether that be in terms of employment or recidivism), and also because of the idealization of prison education as a liberatory practice. A third contributing factor is the limitation on equipment necessary for STEM classes inside prisons. A consequence of this is that the prison classroom can appear the ideal space for re-invigorating traditional modes of learning and, especially, traditional texts. We should be wary of using our most vulnerable students to reinvigorate our field.

Conclusion

In her account of the concept of "restorative impulse," Kay Pranis explains that, while restorative justice tends to focus on an individual who has committed an offense, restorative impulse emphasizes the restoration of communities through recognizing and addressing all kinds of harm, systemic as well as individual (Pranis 2012). That is to say, restorative justice, like the justice system more broadly, holds the individual accountable, while restorative impulse locates account-ability in the community – local, civic, and national. The approach to prison education that I advocate for in this contribution follows Pranis's lead toward centering community as a site both for ac-countability and for generative connection.

Some of the most valuable work that we do as educators working across carceral and non-carceral spaces is build community. Put a group of intellectually hungry individuals in a room together and give them a problem to chew over – be it a metaphor, an equation, sentence construction, or a tragic play – and they have the potential to form connections to one another that produce mutual support, creative energy, and self-reflection. One of the most significant aspects of my early prison teaching experience was witnessing incarcerated college students form a spontaneous closing circle to wrap up our weekly study hall sessions. Between 7:30 and 7:45 on a Friday evening, you could find us seated in a loose circle of school desks, with a student in the middle, performing their poetry. This performance space held a charge that was built through hours of algebraic problems, close reading exercises, and discussions of Latin grammar. The act of working together to solve intellectual challenges fuelled our students in their shared literary output and created a community of support that drew a steady stream of new students to the program. Powerful intellectual community coheres through the sharing of stories. As hooks writes, "it is a ritual of communion that opens our minds and hearts.... Stories help us to connect to a world beyond the self" (hooks 2010, 52–3). Among the riches that Classics offers is an abundance of stories. The strength of the community that took shape through the performance of poems, however, involved the students sharing their own stories and learning, through observation and imitation of one another, how to access their own voices and their inner wisdom. Sometimes they incorporated ancient motifs (or even fragments of Latin texts), but most of the time they did not.

I suggest that we work with these communities in mind, leveraging our cultural capital in Classics, but leaving the stage open for our incarcerated students to shape the programs that they have access to. I also suggest that we take a leaf out of their book and talk to one another, not only through written scholarship and occasional panels, although these formats are important, but also through the intentional sharing of stories, of what has worked well and of where we live with regret, of what keeps us going, and of what causes stress, exhaustion, or fear as we grapple with the carceral system. In order to develop collective practices of self-reflexivity and mutual accountability within the field of Classics prison education, we need collaboration and conversation, both with our students and amongst ourselves.

Notes

1 The initial draft of this contribution was written prior to the impact of COVID-19. As it goes to publication, the world of higher education – in prisons and on college campuses – has radically changed. Some prison education programs are currently on hiatus, while others have switched to a correspondence format (Burke 2020).
2 On the preferred terminology for referring to incarcerated individuals, see the "Letter on Language" by Eddie Ellis (Stern, 2014, xiii-xv): in particular,

Ellis critiques the terms "inmates, convicts, prisoners, and felons" (xiii). See also Castro and Gould, 2019, 3.
3 Lori Gruen, presentation at "The Prison and the Academy: Exploring Critical Prison Pedagogy," Princeton University, April 13, 2018.
4 Thus, the collection of articles in *Critical Education* (volumes 9 and 10) devoted to higher education in prison is subtitled "Beyond Recidivism."
5 Cf. the more general criticisms of critical pedagogy in Ellsworth 1989 and Lather 1991.
6 For example: Theater of War (directed by Bryan Doerries) and The Warrior Chorus (directed by Peter Meineck and Desiree Sanchez), both of which programs use Greek tragedy to work with veterans (see the useful discussion in Adamitis and Gamel 2013, with reference to Shay 1994). See also the use of classical mythology in The Odyssey Project (discussed by Morgan Michael in this volume) and The Medea Project: Theater for Incarcerated Women (directed by Rhodessa Jones), a program that has served not only incarcerated women but also women in various stages of re-entry and women impacted by HIV (Fraden 2001; Rabinowitz 2013; Alexandra Pappas in this volume).
7 The Symposium on Incarceration organized by the Center for Hellenic Studies at Harvard University on 28 February, 2020, exemplifies the kind of cross-disciplinary conversation that is necessary for building the collective practices of critical reflection that I am describing: https://chs.harvard.edu/CHS/article/display/7053.events.
8 Abundant bibliography can be found in the report published on *Pharos* in January 2020, "Report: White Supremacy and the Past and Future of Classics Roundtable." http://pages.vassar.edu/pharos/2020/01/24/report-white-supremacy-and-the-past-and-future-of-classics-roundtable.

Works cited

Adamitis, Jana, and Mary-Kay Gamel. 2013. "Theaters of War." In *Roman Literature, Gender and Reception*, edited by Donald Lateiner, Barbara K. Gold, and Judith Perkins, 284–302. New York and Oxford: Routledge.
Burke, Lilah. 2020. "College Programs in Prisons Go Remote." 18 June, 2020. https://www.insidehighered.com/news/2020/06/18/college-programs-prisons-adapt-covid.
Castro, Erin L., and Michael Brawn. 2017. "Critiquing Critical Pedagogies Inside the Prison Classroom: A Dialogue Between Student and Teacher." *Harvard Educational Review* 87 (1): 99–121.
Castro, Erin L., and Mary R. Gould. 2018. "What Is Higher Education in Prison? Introduction to Radical Departures: Ruminations on the Purposes of Higher Education in Prison." *Critical Education* 9 (10): 2–15.
Castro, Erin L., and Mary R. Gould. 2019. "Higher Education in Prison. Thoughts on Building a Community of Scholarship and Practice." *Critical Education* 10 (13): 1–15.
Corbett, Erin. 2018. "Why Do They Return? Deconstructing the Prison Recidivism Paradigm." https://www.swarthmore.edu/news-events/listen-educator-erin-corbett-99-deconstructing-prison-recidivism-paradigm.

Davis III, James. 2018. "Caught Somewhere Between ..." *Critical Education* 9 (15): 2–12.

Ellsworth, Elizabeth. 1989. "Why Doesn't This Feel Empowering? Working Through the Repressive Myths of Critical Pedagogy." *Harvard Educational Review* 59 (3): 297–325.

Erzen, Tanya, Mary R. Gould, and Jody Lewen. 2019. *Equity and Excellence in Practice: A Guide for Higher Education in Prison*. Alliance for Higher Education in Prison and Prison University Project.

Fraden, Rena. 2001. *Imagining Medea. Rhodessa Jones and Theater for Incarcerated Women*. Chapel Hill: The University of North Carolina Press.

Freire, Paulo. 1968. *Pedagogy of the Oppressed*. New York: Seabury Press.

Goff, Barbara E., ed. 2005. *Classics and Colonialism*. London: Duckworth.

Greenwood, Emily. 2010. *Afro-Greeks: Dialogues between Anglophone Caribbean Literature and Classics in the Twentieth Century*. Oxford: Oxford University Press.

Haley, Shelley. 1993. "Black Feminist Thought and Classics: Re-membering, Re-claiming, Re-empowering." In *Feminist Theory and the Classics*, edited by Nancy Sorkin Rabinowitz and Amy Richlin, 23–43. New York and Oxford: Routledge.

Hall, Budd L., and Rajesh Tandon. 2017. "Decolonization of Knowledge, Epistemicide, Participatory Research and Higher Education." *Research for All* 1 (1): 6–19.

hooks, bell. 1994. *Teaching to Transgress: Education as the Practice of Freedom*. New York and Oxford: Routledge.

hooks, bell. 2010. *Teaching Critical Thinking: Practical Wisdom*. New York and Oxford: Routledge.

Karpowitz, Daniel. 2017. *College in Prison: Reading in an Age of Mass Incarceration*. New Brunswick: Rutgers University Press.

Lather, Patti. 1991. "Post-Critical Pedagogies: A Feminist Reading." *Education and Society* 1 (2): 100–111.

Pompa, Lori. 2013. "One Brick at a Time: The Power and Possibility of Dialogue Across the Prison Wall." *The Prison Journal* 93 (2): 127–134.

Pranis, Kay. 2012. "The Restorative Impulse." *Tikkun* 27 (1). https://www.tikkun.org/the-restorative-impulse.

Rabinowitz, Nancy S. 2013. "Ancient Myth and Feminist Politics: The Medea Project and San Francisco Women's Prisons." In *Roman Literature, Gender and Reception: Domina Illustris*, edited by Donald Lateiner, Barbara K. Gold, and Judith Perkins, 267–283. New York and Oxford: Routledge.

Ram-Prasad, Krishnan. 2019. "Reclaiming the Ancient World: Towards a Decolonized Classics." *Eidolon*. https://eidolon.pub/reclaiming-the-ancient-world-c481fc19c0e3.

Scott, Robert. 2018. "Reducing Recidivism via College-in-Prison: Thoughts on Data Collection, Methodology, and the Question of Purpose." *Critical Education* 9 (18): 2–14.

Shay, Jonathan. 1994. *Achilles in Vietnam: Combat Trauma and the Undoing of Character.* Toronto; New York: Atheneum.

Stern, Kaia. 2014. *Voices from American Prisons: Faith, Education, and Healing.* Cambridge, MA: Harvard University Press.

Umachandran, Mathura. 2019. "More Than a Common Tongue: Dividing Race and Classics Across the Atlantic." *Eidolon.* https://eidolon.pub/more-than-a-common-tongue-cfd7edeb6368.

Vasunia, Phiroze. 2013. *The Classics and Colonial India.* Oxford: Oxford University Press.

Wright, Jessica. 2017. "Latin Behind Bars: Teaching College Latin in an American Prison." *Eidolon.* https://eidolon.pub/latin-behind-bars-8ab9cfb14557.

Index

For Product Safety Concerns and Information please contact our EU
representative GPSR@taylorandfrancis.com
Taylor & Francis Verlag GmbH, Kaufingerstraße 24, 80331 München, Germany